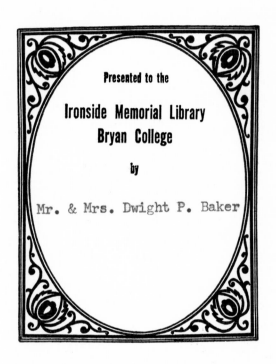

# BLACK AFRICAN LITERATURE in English Since 1952

# BLACK AFRICAN LITERATURE
## in English
## Since 1952
### WORKS AND CRITICISM

JOHNSON REPRINT CORPORATION
NEW YORK      •      LONDON
1967

by BARBARA ABRASH
Russell Sage College Library

with an introduction by
JOHN F. POVEY,
Associate Professor, University of California at Los Angeles
Chairman of the African Language and Literature Committee,
African Studies Association of America

Printed in the United States of America

# INTRODUCTION

The colonial powers may have much to answer for in Africa, but when they quit that continent they left a vital gift--their languages. With few exceptions, the languages of Africa are incredibly varied in form and limited in their geographic extent. Linguists are still not even certain of the number of languages that may be spoken on that continent. Some, like Hausa or Swahili, extend across wide geographic areas; others are used by very small tribal groups. The fragmentation that this brings within the boundaries of the newly established independent nations of Africa is sufficient impetus to the need to find a lingua franca. The language chosen is usually the ex-colonial tongue, for the foreign administrations had welded their language deeply into the social structures of government, of administration, and above all of higher education. Besides this national function the adopted language serves a vital international purpose. French, and even more, English, gives these new nations their access to the outside world. The strength

I

of America and the far flung residue of British power in its
Commonwealth has decided that English will be the most pre-
dominant and extensive resource for international communication.  For many Africans English is the vehicle for international trade, for developing technology and for the political controversy of United Nations debate.

An interesting aspect of the use of the European languages in Africa is the relatively new development of
national literatures in several countries on the continent.
Such writing uses the forms and language borrowed from
abroad, while it draws upon the content of local African
experience and culture.  The use of a European language
for literary expression was initially tried by French West
African writers.  During the thirties, Aime Cesaire and
now President, Leopold Senghor, met in Paris with American
Negro poets living abroad, especially Langston Hughes and
Claude McKay.  Their interaction generated a surge of im-
pressive, if occasionally rhetorical, poetry and some subtle
and witty novels.  Birago Diop and David Diop, Mongo Betti
and Camara Laye were among those whose work formed the
brilliant first fruits of that now famous concept
"negritude."  This philosophy creates mixed reactions.
There is admiration for its urgent challenge to oppression

and to those false concepts of progress that derive from
assimilation policies. There is respect for the fervent and
humane pleas in such lines as these from the poetry of
Senghor.

> Let us cry 'here' at the rebirth of the world.
> Like the yeast which white flour needs.
> For who else would teach rhythm to a dead world
> of machines and guns. (Prayer to Masks.)

Negritude had, however, other implications which made the
Defense Legitime of the first proud African manifesto seem
less legitimate. There was Diop's praise for "those who
have invented nothing" and Senghor's twisted vision of the
American Negro airmen as god's avengers upon white Europe.
These may have been necessary excesses in making a first
assertion of the dignity of the Negro and the worth of his
culture and belief. Such declarations cleared the way for
others to follow without the occasional over-assertion.
Soyinka's witty remark that a tiger does not have to pro-
claim his "tigritude" may represent a luxury allowed him by
the different political history which confronts him as he
writes. Soyinka is a generation after Senghor; the generation that knows African independence, not the struggle to

achieve it.

French African writing begins with the fiery declarations propounded in the cafes, but English language writing began with that unexpected haphazardness of which the English love modestly to boast. The initial work of this new literature in English from Africa came with the publication of Amos Tutuola's first and still most famous novel, The Palm Wine Drinkard. The book has stirred some controversy, for Tutuola's knowledge of English, like his formal education, is very limited. His London publishers printed his work without much grammatical correction, for it was felt that alteration would have destroyed the instinctive and charming quality of his story-telling. The novel's weirdly unlettered style caused Europeans, the poet Dylan Thomas among them, to find in this work a primitive natural poetry. Many Africans thought it would only confirm the prejudiced European view of African writing as quaint and incompetent. As a matter of act, both attitudes are possibly true. Tutuola remains indifferent to both sides of the debate and has continued to write several other books in this literally inimitable style.

Interesting as Tutuola may be, it was not in such exotic work that the true quality of African literature was going to expose itself.  In 1958 Chinua Achebe published <u>Things</u> <u>Fall Apart</u>, the first novel of his tetralogy.  This work reflected a very different caliber of writing and was the forerunner to a number of other significant books written by a group of young Nigerians.  In the early fifties at Ibadan University College, a number of highly gifted young men attended class together.  Their relationship seems to have touched off a spark that ignited each other's individual skills.  Now the names, Wole Soyinka, J. P. Clark, Christopher Okigbo, along with Chinua Achebe, have become the most significant contemporary African writers with whom this bibliography concerns itself.  These writers have little in common with the efforts of Tutuola, for they are cosmopolitan and highly literate men, studied academically in English literature and as aware of current experimental trends in the poetry and drama in English as would be any young writer in this country.  One can point to the influence of Ezra Pound on Okigbo and of Hopkins on Clark.  One can demonstrate how Achebe draws upon the novels of Hardy and Soyinka upon the plays of Synge.  These writers are eclectic as they develop their personal idioms.

Such a critical observation brings one to the most significant fact about this new writing, that it is an attempted synthesis which brings together two disparate traditions into a new and expressive unity. Such writing shows an awareness of the range of styles in contemporary English literature and it experiments with the means by which they can be adapted to fulfill a new purpose. That purpose is the explication and assertion of the African culture and sentiment, the cultural roots that are sustaining these young writers in their lands. Yet the double element in their writing is only evidence of another more personal dualism that exists in the writer himself for he is simultaneously African, yet trained in the western concepts of literary art. The inner debate to which they must all be prone is explored in a beautiful poem by Gabriel Okara, who debates the double thread of his experience and concludes with the following stanza which exposes his dilemma.

> And I lost in the morning mist
> of an age at a riverside keep
> wandering in the mystic rhythm
> of jungle drums and the concerto.
> (Piano and Drums)

The fact that this new literature from Africa draws from the English tradition has had a very important effect upon its reception abroad. Until this time, African literature

---if it can properly even be called by that term---was
largely denied to outsiders. The fact that the tradition
was an oral one and the barriers imposed by the use of
languages few could comprehend, made it doubly unlikely
that an American reader would be acquainted with this rich
source. Even where collection and translation made such
literature available to us, the resulting poetry did not
accommodate itself to our standards. The, to us, unnatural
stylistic devices of rhetorical repetition and the unexpected comparisons, revealed a culture so different from ours
that the effort of understanding could only be sustained
through the illumination of the anthropologists. We could,
it appeared, approach this writing not as literature but
as a revelation of social custom which the folk-lore
specialists had described.

The writers' decision to use the English language, not
as a translation but as a direct line of communication to
the international audience, changed this, for the language
made such writing readily approachable to the outsider.
This material was the more easily available because so
much of it was published in London first. There were sub-
sequent paper-backed editions which sold extensively on the
African market, but the audience remains essentially a

double one, part African, part international. There may be
a deceptive universality in much of this writing, for
language may conceal considerable differences of attitude.
A person asked to give his impression of a mask made by a
Yoruba carver might well admit himself incapable of judg-
ing something so far from his experience. The same person
would not have any inhibitions in commenting upon a play
written by a Yoruba dramatist in English--for that comprehension is expected automatically by virtue of the
language used. The more aware critic realizes the possible limitation in his response to this exciting new
literature. Its surface meaning is clear, because he
understands the language and is aware of the influences
which are imposing themselves from his own literature.
Yet he might acknowledge an inadequacy. It is not that
the vocabulary is difficult. It is not hard to elucidate
what kind of cattle are the <u>Fulani</u> <u>Cattle</u>, written by
J. P. Clark. It is easy to gain sufficient knowledge of
Ijaw belief in the significance of <u>Abiku</u> to appreciate the
tender tone of that Clark poem so entitled. But at a
deeper level we must approach cautiously, for how can
we be sure that our comprehension is adequate to the
event, or that our response is close to that intended by

the African writer and not distracted by our own cultural
assumptions and prejudices? We must read this work with
care and sympathy, for through it we gain insight into
the new African becoming westernized in some sense, and
yet born to a tradition that is an indivisible part of
his consciousness.

This new writing has become of considerable interest
in America. Not only are there formal courses given at
several American universities, but a number of high
school teachers have attempted to introduce a novel or
a play from Africa into their syllabus to indicate to
their students the range of human experience. The developing internationalism in the outlook of America,
which is reflected in some of the recent changes in
education, can well be served by the new writers in
English. Many inter-disciplinary programs are being
constructed and presented around an area focal point
and for these the discovery of such a literature is all
important. These writers can open the world of Africa
directly to the eyes of American students. They become
the window through which we see the new Africa in the
words of the most able and responsive of its young
men. Not by the explanations of the anthropologists,

but from the directly conceived experiences, we learn of
the nature of the change in modern Africa. No one who has
read No Longer at Ease can fail to understand the pressures
which are imposed upon the young educated African. No one
can read Weep Not Child without seeing in a new light the
African struggle for independence and individual dignity
in the face of the quicksand of social and political change.

Where the teacher is concerned only to introduce a
single novel into the classroom, little more is needed
than to win the American publisher to the potential of
this new market. But those who wish to pursue studies
more deeply in African literature require a formal appa-
ratus of scholarship; need bibliographical references and
lists. It is this demand Mrs. Abrash has fulfilled so
well and for the first time. It may seem surprising that
such a work is needed when this present bibliography lists
several others already completed. But the other bibliographies have defects in their organization for the purpose
of the scholar. Earlier publications will remain of value
--for all the bibliographies cover some unfamiliar and
separate ground. Mrs. Abrash's work is unique in that it
is conceived in terms of the American student, makes references to American publications, and can be the necessary

tool in the classrooms where such material is being taught.
When the committee of which I am chairman heard about the
work of Mrs. Abrash, we recognized its valuable quality,
and did everything possible to suggest our interest and
support. The other bibliographies had not served our purpose and only something conceived in the manner of this
present study would be suitable for the needs of the
American colleges.

There have been other significant lists. Mrs. Margaret
Amosu, the librarian of the University at Ibadan, had pro-
duced a useful "Preliminary Bibliography" which covers a
great deal of ground. As an early attempt, this work has
been invaluable; yet the limitations are clearly admitted
by the writer herself. There are numerous titles with
such minimal references that they must presumably be listed
only by report. The attempt to cover all African literature in all languages and to report on the enormous range
of South African writing promises an extent that cannot
be sustained bibliographically. The range of Mr. Ramsaran's
study is even wider, for it takes Carribean and American
Negro work as part of its composite, besides all the published range of African languages. Most valuable are the
introductory comments and the wealth of material, but it

is not so specific and exhaustive as the American student would require. We anticipated that such an exhaustive study would have been achieved by Jahnheinz Jahn when his profound bibliography was published last year. It is a work of great scholarship, for no one has read so widely and industriously as Jahn in this field. Yet for all its range of Negro writing across the Carribean and Africa and America, there was a curious selection policy which derives from Jahn's questionable thesis of an African Geist. His is a bibliography of "neo-African literature" and works that apparently did not reflect this neo-African spirit appropriately were disregarded. For all its great extent and the amount of new information it offers, his arbitrary choice gives the bibliography in the final analysis only partial nature. Most valuable to date have been the more limited and detailed efforts of Mrs. Porter, the librarian of Howard University, who has combined a librarian's precision with a skilled knowledge of the field. But last year when the ASA Literature Committee was formed, there was no one single comprehensive scholarly bibliography .

The committee saw at once that a satisfactory bibliography was the first need for any formal development of

African Literature studies in this country. It was the English language literature that concerned us most at first. African vernacular literature was being listed by Professor Daniel Kunene, but his task was likely to be a long and complex process because of the language difficulties involved. We felt that the French, through <u>Presence Africain</u> had done a better job than the English in maintaining adequate lists. But it was for English language literature that the need was greatest, and the more so in that it was most likely this very area that would have the first and most obvious appeal to American teachers and students. It seems to me that Mrs. Abrash's bibliography has impressively fulfilled our urgent need. It has the completeness and accuracy that comes when a librarian has worked with all her technique in a specific and exhaustive manner. It lists the major writers, their works, and the most important and most available critical writings upon their work. Another invaluable aspect is the listing of places where some of these writers are anthologized. Often the only way of gaining a comprehensive sense of the work of these men is to trace their work in anthologies. This makes such a listing of a special value to students undertaking research papers in this area, for publication has not always been easy for the African writers and some have had to disperse their stories and poems very widely in magazines.

I believe that this bibliography is an important step in the academic study of African literature in this country. At last there is a list that is formal, functional and scholarly. It will be invaluable to those committed to the field and it will also indicate to others the possibilities to be derived from its study. It will be necessary to keep this valuable list up to date. We are making plans to do so. But this work, as it stands, will, I believe, be definitive for scholarly purposes, for it is so precisely geared to the needs of our colleges that it will remain a standard reference. We have occasion to be grateful to Mrs. Abrash for her work.

John Povey,
Associate Professor of English, UCLA
Chairman of the African Language and
    Literature Committee
African Studies Association of America

# Preface

This is a listing of creative works of literature in English by black African writers, along with relevant criticism. The publication of Amos Tutuola's <u>Palm-wine drinkard</u> is taken as the starting point, although earlier publications of currently productive writers are included.

Some children's books have been included, but there has been no attempt at a comprehensive listing. Dialect literature generally does not fall within the scope of this list. Essays and autobiographies deemed to be of literary interest, as well as a few plays which have been performed but which have not been published, are included. Critical writings are mainly from publications readily available in academic libraries.

The list is organized in the following order:
1. Bibliographies.
2. Criticism: books.
3. Criticism: journal articles, arranged by subject.
4. Anthologies, listed under compiler.
5. Alphabetical author listing.
    a. Full-length works listed alphabetically by title; reviews (arranged chronologically) follow each work.
    b. Short stories published in periodicals.
    c. Anthologies in which the author's work appears.
    d. General critical articles on an individual author.
6. Selected periodicals.
7. Index to authors of creative and critical writing. Book reviewers are not included.


Troy, N. Y.                                         B.A.

# TABLE OF CONTENTS

Bibliographies . . . . . . . . . . . . . . . Page  1

Criticism:  Books . . . . . . . . . . . . . Page  3

              Articles . . . . . . . . . . Page  5

Anthologies . . . . . . . . . . . . . . . . Page 21

Authors . . . . . . . . . . . . . . . . . . Page 26

Periodicals . . . . . . . . . . . . . . . . Page 86

Index . . . . . . . . . . . . . . . . . . . Page 88

## Bibliographies

1. Amosu, Margaret. A preliminary bibliography of creative African
   writing in the European languages. Special supplement to
   African Notes, Bulletin of the Institute of African Studies.
   Ibadan: University of Ibadan, 1964. v, 35p.

2. Jahn, Janheinz. A bibliography of neo-African literature
   from Africa, America and the Caribbean. New York: Praeger,
   1965; London: Deutsch, 1965. xxxv, 359p.

   Rev: M.M. Mahood, J. of Modern African Studies, III, 4
       (December 1965), 640-645.
       John Povey, Africa Report, XI, 3 (March 1966), 45.

3. Porter, Dorothy. "African and Caribbean creative writings:
   a bibliographic survey," African Forum, I, 4 (Spring 1966),
   107-111.

4. --. "Fiction by African authors: a preliminary checklist,"
   African Studies Bulletin, V, 2 (May 1962), 54-66.

5. --. "Notes on some African writers," Africa and the United
   States: images and realities. U.S. National Commission
   for UNESCO. 8th National Conference, Boston, October 22-26,
   1961. Washington, D.C.: Department of State Publication
   7332, 1961 (African Series 26), p.165-173.

6. --, ed. A catalogue of the African collection in the Moorland
   Foundation, Howard University Library, compiled by students
   in the Program of African Studies. Washington, D.C.:
   Howard University Press, 1958. 398p.

   --. "Supplement to the catalogue of the African collection
   in the Moorland Foundation of the Howard University Library,"
   compiled by H.P. Alexander. MLS thesis. Washington, D.C.:
   Catholic University, 1963. 106p.

7. Ramsaran, John A. New approaches to African literature.
    Ibadan: Ibadan University Press, 1965. 177p.


Note: The Journal of Commonwealth Literature includes
      comprehensive annual bibliographies of creative
      African writing in English.

Criticism and interpretation: Books

8. Abraham, William E. Mind of Africa. London: Weidenfeld and
   Nicolson, 1962; Chicago: University of Chicago, 1962.
   206p. Chicago: Phoenix Books, 1966.

   Rev: Dennis Duerden, J. of Modern African Studies, I, 1
          (March 1963), 115-116.
          Abiola Irele, Presence Africaine, Eng. ed., XX, 48
          (1963), 217-220.
          L. Bloom, Contrast, II, 3 (1963-64), 82-85.
          A. Mazrui, Makerere Journal, 9 (1964), 84-85.
          TLS, 16 September 1965, p.812.

9. Beier, Ulli, ed. Introduction to African literature. Evanston:
   Northwestern University Press, 1967; London: Longmans, 1967.
   288p.

10. Bown, Lalage, and Michael Crowder, eds. First International
    Congress of Africanists. Proceedings. Accra, 11-18 December
    1962. Foreword K. Onwuka Dike. Evanston: Northwestern
    University Press, 1964; London: published for the
    International Congress of Africanists by Longmans, 1964.
    xi, 368p.

11. Gleason, Judith Illsley. This Africa: novels by West Africans
    in English and French. Evanston: Northwestern University
    Press, 1965. xix, 186p. Bibliography: p.178-186.

    Rev: M.M. Mahood, J. of Modern African Studies, III, 4
          (December 1965), 640-645.
          TLS, 30 December 1965, p.1209.
          J. Povey, Phylon, XXVII, 1 (Spring 1966), 105-106.

12. Jahn, Janheinz. Muntu: an outline of the new African culture,
    trans. Marjorie Grene. New York: Grove, 1961; London:
    Faber, 1961. 267p. Bibliography: p.252-259.

    Rev: Omidiji Aragbalu, Black Orpheus, 6 (1959), 57.
          Gerhard Kubik, Black Orpheus, 9 (1961), 63-65.

13. Moore, Gerald. Seven African writers [L.S. Senghor, David Diop,
    Camara Laye, Amos Tutuola, Chinua Achebe, Mongo Beti,
    Ezekiel Mphahlele]. London: Oxford University Press (Three
    Crowns Book), 1962. xx, 108p. Bibliography: p.103-108.

    Rev: Omidiji Aragbalu, Black Orpheus, 13 (1963), 57-58.
        Clive Wake, Contrast, II, 2 (1963), 97-100.
        David Rubadiri, J. of Modern African Studies, I, 3
        (1963), 419-420.
        Presence Africaine, Eng. ed., XVII, 45 (1963), 220-221.
        TLS, 5 April 1963, p.234.
        Christina Aidoo, Transition, III, 10 (1963), 45-46.

14. --, ed. African literature and the universities, ed., with an
    introduction by Gerald Moore. Ibadan: published for the
    Congress for Cultural Freedom by Ibadan University Press,
    1965. iv, 148p.

    Rev: J. Povey, J. of Commonwealth Literature, 2 (December
        1966), 164-167.

15. Mphahlele, Ezekiel. The African image. London: Faber, 1962;
    New York: Praeger, 1962. 240p. Bibliography: p.227-229.

    Rev: Philip Segal, Contrast, II, 1 (1962), 7-14.
        Abiola Irele, Presence Africaine, Eng. ed., XVI, 44
        (1962), 231-234.
        T.R.M. Creighton, J. of Modern African Studies, I,
        1 (March 1963), 117-118.

16. Nicol, Davidson S.H. Africa, a subjective view. London:
    Longmans, 1964; Cambridge: Harvard University Press, 1964.
    88p. London: Longmans (Forum Series), 1965.

17. Press, John, ed. Commonwealth literature: unity and diversity
    in a common culture. Extracts from the proceedings of a
    conference held at Bodington Hall, Leeds, 9-12 September
    1964, under the auspices of the University of Leeds. London:
    Heinemann, 1965. 223p.

    Rev: V.S. Naipaul, New Statesman, 24 September 1965,
        p.452-453.
        John Povey, Transition, V, 23 (1965), 50-51.

18. Ramsaran, John A. New approaches to African literature; a
    guide to Negro-African writing and related studies. Ibadan:
    Ibadan University Press, 1965. v, 177p. Includes
    bibliographies.

    Rev: M.M. Mahood, J. of Modern African Studies, III,
        4 (December 1965), 640-645.
        Eldred Jones, Bulletin of the Association for African
        Literature in English, 4 (1966), 41.


19. Ramsaran, John A., and Janheinz Jahn. Approaches to African
    literature: non-English writings, by Janheinz Jahn and
    English writing in West Africa, by John Ramsaran. Includes
    bibliographies. Ibadan: Ibadan University Press, 1959.
    31p.


20. Wauthier, Claude. The literature and thought of modern Africa,
    trans. Shirley Kay. New York: Praeger, 1967; London:
    Pall Mall, 1966. 323p. Includes bibliography.


Criticism and Interpretation: Articles.


AFRICAN LITERATURE


## General

21. Achebe, Chinua. "The black writer's burden," Presence Africaine,
    Eng. ed., XXXI, 59 (1966), 135-140.

22. --. "The role of the writer in a new nation," Nigerian
    Libraries, I, 3 (September 1964), 113-119; Nigeria Magazine,
    81 (1964), 157-160.

23. "Africa on record," TLS, 11 June 1964, p.501-502.

24. "Are there underdeveloped writers?" TLS, 27 May 1965, p.429-430.

25. Astrachan, A.M. "Creative writing," Nigeria Magazine, 79
    (1963), 290-294.

26. Awoonor-Williams, George. "Fresh vistas for African literature,"
    African Review (Accra), I, 1 (May 1965), 35, 38.

27. Banham, Martin. "The beginnings of a Nigerian Literature in English," Review of English Literature, III, 2 (April 1962), 88-99.

28. --. "A piece that we may fairly call our own," Ibadan, 12 (June 1961), 15-18.

29. --, and John Ramsaran. "West African writing," Books Abroad, XXXVI, 4 (Autumn 1962), 371-374. Includes bibliography.

30. "Black out," TLS, 10 May 1963, p.341. [On censorship in S. Africa.]

31. Bodurin, A. "What is African literature?" African Statesman, I, 1 (October-December 1965), 33-42.

32. Crowder, Michael. "Tradition and change in Nigerian literature," Bulletin of the Association for African Literature in English, 3 (1965), 1-17.

33. --. "Tradition and change in Nigerian literature," Triquarterly, 5 (1966), 117-128. Includes bibliography.

34. Dathorne, O.R. "Writing from Nigeria," Bulletin of the Association for African Literature in English, 2 (n.d.), 31-32.

35. Dei-Anang, M.F. "A writer's outlook," Okyeame, I (January 1961), 40-43.

36. deMott, Benjamin. "Oyiemu-o?" American Scholar, XXXII, 2 (Spring 1963), 292-306.

37. "East African new writing," special issue, East Africa Journal (January 1967). David Rubadiri, guest editor.

38. Echeruo, M.J.C. "Incidental fiction in Nigeria," African Writer, I, 1 (August 1962), 10-11.

39. Ekwensi, Cyprian. "African literature," Nigeria Magazine, 83 (1964), 294-299.

40. --. "Literary influences on a young Nigerian," TLS, 4 June 1964, p.475-476.

41. --. "Problems of Nigerian writers," Nigeria Magazine, 78 (1963), 217-219.

42. Gleason, Judith. "Out of the irony of words," Transition, IV,
    18 (1965), 34-38.

43. Hanshell, Deryck. "African writing today," Month, XXXII
    (November 1964), 246-254.

44. Haresnape, Geoffrey. "The literary picture in South Africa,"
    Books Abroad, XXXIX, 1 (Winter 1965), 32-34.

45. Hopkinson, Tom. "Deaths and entrances: the emergence of African
    writing," Twentieth Century, CLXV, 986 (April 1959), 332-342.

46. Jahn, Janheinz. "African literature," Presence Africaine,
    Eng. ed., XX, 48 (1963), 47-57.

47. --, and John Ramsaran. "Approaches to African literature,"
    WALA News, III 3 (June 1959), 117-128.

48. Jones, D.A.N. "Jombo," New Statesman, 29 January 1965, p.164.
    [Review of several Nigerian literary works.]

49. Jones, Eldred. "Jungle drums and wailing piano: West African
    fiction and poetry in English," African Forum, I, 4 (Spring
    1966), 93-106.

50. --. "Nationalism and the writer," Commonwealth literature,
    John Press, ed. London: Heinemann, 1965, p.151-156.

51. Jordan, A.C. "Towards an African literature," Africa South,
    I, 4 (1957), cont. through IV, 3 (1960). [A series of
    twelve articles.]

52. July, Robert W. "African literature and the African personality,"
    Black Orpheus, 14 (1964), 33-45.

53. Kane, Mohamadou. "The African writer and his public," Presence
    Africaine, Eng. ed., XXX, 58 (1966), 10-32.

54. Killam, Douglas. "Recent African fiction," Bulletin of the
    Association for African Literature in English, 2 (n.d.), 1-10.

55. Lienhardt, Peter. "Tribesmen and cosmopolitans: on African
    literature," Encounter, XXV, 5 (November 1965), 54-57.

56. Lindfors, Bernth. "African vernacular styles in Nigerian fiction,"
    CLA Journal, IX, 3 (March 1966), 265-273.

57.  --. "Post-war literature in English by African writers from
     South Africa:  a study of the effects of environment upon
     literature," Phylon, XXVII, 1 (Spring 1966), 50-62.

58.  "The literary drought," East Africa Journal, II, 10 (March
     1966), 11-15.  [Discussion of East African literature:
     G. Moore, E. Mphahlele, Okot p'Bitek, R. Neogy.]

59.  "Literature as symptom?" TLS, 11 January 1963, p.25.

60.  lo Liyong, Taban.  "Can we correct literary barrenness in
     East Africa?" East Africa Journal (December 1966), 5-13.

61.  Mathew, Gervase.  "The literature of Africa," New Blackfriars,
     46 (October 1964), 41-43.

62.  Moore, Gerald.  "African writing seen from Salisbury,"
     Presence Africaine, Eng. ed., III, 31 (1960), 87-94.

63.  --. "English words, African lives," Presence Africaine,
     Eng. ed., XXVI, 54 (1965), 90-101.

64.  --, and Donald Stuart.  "African literature, French and English,"
     Makerere Journal, 8 (1963), 29-34.

65.  Mphahlele, Ezekiel.  "African literature for beginners," Africa
     Today, XIV, 1 (January 1967), 25-31.

66.  --. "Black and white," New Statesman, 10 September 1960,
     p.342-346.

67.  --. "The language of African literature," Harvard Educational
     Review, XXXIV, 2 (Spring 1964), 298-306.

68.  --. "Writers in search of themes," West African Review,
     XXXII, 416 (August 1962), 40-41.

69.  Nakasa, Nathaniel.  "Writing in South Africa," Classic, I, 1
     (1963), 56-63.

70.  "Nation to nation," TLS, 15 March 1963, p.177.

71.  Nazareth, Peter.  "The African writer and commitment," (letter)
     Transition, IV, 19 (1965), 6-7.

72. "New East African writing," special issue, East African Journal (September 1966). Ezekiel Mphahlele, guest editor.

73. Nicol, Abioseh. "Negritude in West Africa," New Statesman, 10 September 1960, p.353-354.

74. --. "The soft pink palms," Presence Africaine, Eng. ed., 8-10 (1956), 107-121.

75. Nkosi, Lewis. "African fiction: Part I - South Africa: protest," Africa Report, VII, 9 (October 1962), 3-6.

76. --. "African literature: Part II - English-speaking West Africa," Africa Report, VII, 11 (December 1962), 15-17.

77. --. "Against the tribe," New African, IV, 3 (May 1965), 70-71.

78. --. "Annals of apartheid," New Statesman, 29 January 1965, p.164-165.

79. --. "Fiction by black South Africans," Black Orpheus, 19 (1966), 48-54.

80. --. "Some conversations with African writers," Africa Report, IX, 7 (July 1964), 7-21.

81. --. "Where does African literature go from here?" Africa Today, XI, 9 (December 1966), 7-11.

82. Obumselu, Ben. "The background of modern African literature," Ibadan, 22 (June 1966), 46-59.

83. Okara, Gabriel. "African speech - English words," Transition, III, 10 (1963), 15-16.

84. Okot, p'Bitek. "The self in African imagery," Transition, IV, 15 (1964), 32-

85. Partridge, A.C. "Recent trends in South African English writing," English, XV, 90 (Autumn 1965), 235-237.

86. Povey, John. "Contemporary West African writing in English," Books Abroad, XL, 3 (Summer 1966), 253-260.

87. --. "How do you make a course in African literature?" Transition, IV, 18 (1965), 39-42.

88. Ramsaran, John A. "Literature in West Africa and the West Indies," West African Review (July 1961). Reprint: Negro Digest (March 1962).

89. --, and Martin Banham. "West African writing," Books Abroad, XXXVI, 4 (Autumn 1962), 371-374. Includes bibliography.

90. --, and Janheinz Jahn. "Approaches to African literature," WALA News, III, 3 (June 1959), 117-128.

91. Redding, Saunders. "Modern African literature," CLA Journal, VII, 3 (March 1964), 191-201.

92. Rubadiri, David. "Why African literature," Transition, IV, 15 (1964), 39-42.

93. Senanu, K.E. "The literature of West Africa," The Commonwealth pen, A.L. McLeod, ed. Ithaca: Cornell University Press, 1961, p.229-230.

94. Shelton, Austin J. "Behavior and cultural value in West African stories: literary sources for the study of culture contact," Africa, XXXIV (1964), 353-359.

95. --. "Some problems of inter-communication," J. of Modern African Studies, II, 3 (1964), 395-403.

96. --. "Ewo!" Transition, V, 20 (1965), 7-9.

97. "Something new out of Africa," TLS, 6 March 1959, p.131.

98. Soyinka, Wole. "From a common back cloth: a reassessment of the African literary image," American Scholar, XXXII, 3 (Summer 1963), 387-396. Reprint: AMSAC Newsletter, VI, 6.

99. Sterling, Thomas. "Africa's black writers," Holiday Magazine. XLI, 2 (February 1967), 131-140.

100. Wake, Clive H. "African literary criticism," Comparative Literature Studies, I, 3 (1964), 197-205.

101. Wali, Obiajunwa. "The dead end of African literature?" Transition, III, 10 (1963), 13-15.

102. Whiteley, Wilfred H. "The concept of an African prose literature," Diogenes, 37 (Spring 1962), 28-49.

103. "Who reads it?" TLS, 16 September 1965, p.801.

104. "Writing in West Africa; a chance to adapt and to experiment," TLS, 10 August 1962, p.570-571.

## Drama

105. Banham, Martin J. "Drama in the Commonwealth: Nigeria," New Theatre Magazine, 4 (July 1960), 18-21.

106. --. "Notes on Nigerian theatre: 1966," Bulletin of the Association for African Literature in English, 4 (1966), 31-36.

107. Clark, John Pepper. "Aspects of Nigerian drama," Nigeria Magazine, 89 (1966), 118-126.

108. Dathorne, O.R. "Pioneer African drama: heroines and the church," Bulletin of the Association for African Literature in English, 4 (1966), 19-23.

109. deGraft, J.C. "Drama workshop, 1963," Okyeame, II, 1 (1964), 48-50.

110. Esslin, Martin. "Two African playwrights," Black Orpheus, 19 (1966), 33-39. [Clark and Soyinka]

111. Kennard, Peter. "Recent African drama," Bulletin of the Association for African Literature in English, 2 (n.d.), 11-18.

112. Kolade, Christopher. "Looking at drama in Nigeria," African Forum, I, 3 (Winter 1966), 77-79.

113. McHardy, Cecile. "The performing arts in Ghana," African Forum, I, 1 (Summer 1965), 113-117.

114. Ogunba, Oyin. "Theatre in Nigeria," Presence Africaine, Eng. ed., XXX, 58 (1966), 63-88.

115. Reckord, Barry. "Notes on two Nigerian playwrights," New African, IV, 7 (September 1965) 171. [Soyinka and Clark]

116. Shore, Herbert. "Drums, dances and then some," _Texas Quarterly_, VII, 2 (Summer 1964), 225-231.


## Novel

117. Achebe, Chinua. "The novelist as teacher," _Commonwealth Literature_, John Press, ed. London: Heinemann, 1965, p.201-205. Reprint: _New Statesman_, 29 January 1965, p.161-162.

118. Chukwukere, B.I. "African novelists and social change," _Phylon_, XXVI, 3 (Fall 1965), 228-239.

119. Dathorne, O.R. "The African novel - document to experiment," _Bulletin of the Association for African Literature in English_, 3 (1965), 18-39.

120. --. "Document and imagination," _New African_, V, 3 (April 1966), 57-59.

121. Drayton, Arthur D. "The return to the past in the Nigerian novel," _Ibadan_, 10 (1960), 27-30.

122. Edwards, Paul, and David R. Carroll. "Approach to the novel in West Africa," _Phylon_, XXIII, 4 (Winter 1962), 319-331.

123. --. "The novel in West Africa," _Overseas Quarterly_, 3 (June 1963), 176-177.

124. Gerard, Albert S. "The neo-African novel," _Africa Report_, IX, 7 (July 1964), 3-5.

125. Gordimer, Nadine. "The novel and the nation in South Africa," _TLS_, 11 August 1961, p.520-523.

126. Lindfors, Bernth. "Five Nigerian novels," _Books Abroad_, XXXIX, 4 (Autumn 1965), 411-413. Includes bibliographies.

127. --. "Form and technique in the novels of Richard Rive and Alex La Guma," _J. of the New African Literature_, 2 (Fall 1966), 10-15.

128. --. "Nigerian novels of 1965," _Africa Report_, XI, 6 (June 1966), 68-69.

129. Parry, J. "Nigerian novelists," _Contemporary Review_, CC (1961), 377-381.

130. Povey, John F. "Changing themes in the Nigerian novel," J. of the New African Literature, 1 (Spring 1966), 3-11.

131. Reed, John. "Between two worlds: some notes on the presentation by African novelists of the individual in modern African society," Makerere J., 7 (1963), 1-14.

132. Staniland, Martin. "Apartheid and the novel," New African, IV, 1 (March 1965), 15-17.

133. Treadgold, Mary. "Writers in search of themes," West African Review, XXXII, 413 (May 1962), 57-61.

134. Tucker, Martin. "Color and guilt," Africa Today, XII, 2 (February 1965), 13-15.

135. --. "Three West African novels," Africa Today, XII, 9 (November 1965), 10-14.

136. --. "West African literature: the second decade," Africa Today, XIII, 5 (May 1966), 7-9; XIII, 6 (June 1966), 7-8.

137. Wali, Obiajunwa. "The individual and the novel in Africa," Transition, IV, 18 (1965), 31-33.
    Letter: B. Ibe Chukwukere, "That wet-eared new graduate...," Transition, V, 23 (1965), 7-8.

## Poetry

138. Abasiekong, Daniel. "Poetry pure and applied: Rabearivelo and Brutus," Transition, V, 23 (1965), 45-48.

139. Beier, Ulli. "The conflict of cultures in West African poetry," Black Orpheus, 1 (1957), 17-21.

140. --. "Contemporary African poetry in English," Makerere J., II, 4 (1962).

141. --. "Some Nigerian poets," Presence Africaine, Eng. ed., IV-V, 32-33 (1960), 50-63.

142. --. "Three Mbari poets," Black Orpheus, 12 (1963), 46-50.
    [Okigbo, Brutus and Clark]

143. Bilen, Max. "The African poet as bard of his people," Presence Africaine, Eng. ed., XXVI, 54 (1965), 141-145.

144. Butler, Guy. "The English poet in South Africa," Listener, 24 May 1956, p.680-631.

145. Clark, John Pepper. "Another kind of poetry," Transition, V, 25 (1966), 17-25.

146. --. "A note on Nigerian poetry," Presence Africaine, Eng. ed., XXX, 58 (1966), 55-64.

147. --. "Poetry in Africa today," Transition, IV, 18 (1965), 20-26.

148. --. "Themes of African poetry of English expression," Presence Africaine, Eng. ed., XXVI, 54 (1965), 70-89.

149. Echeruo, M.J.C. "Traditional and borrowed elements in Nigerian poetry," Nigeria Magazine, 89 (1966), 142-155.

150. Ferguson, John. "Nigerian poetry in English," English, XV, 90 (Autumn 1965), 231-235.

151. Mezu, S. Okechukwu. "The origins of African poetry," J. of the New African Literature, 2 (Fall 1966), 16-23.

152. Moore, Gerald. "Time and experience in African poetry," Transition VI, 26 (1966), 18-22.

153. Nicol, Davidson. "West African poetry," Africa South in Exile, V, 3 (1961), 115-122.

154. Soyinka, Wole. "And after the narcissist?" African Forum, I, 4 (Spring 1966), 53-64.

155. Theroux, Paul. "Voices out of the skull," Black Orpheus, 20 (1966).

156. Thomas, Peter. "Students and the art of poetry," New African, V, 7 (September 1966), 144-145.

157. Tolson, Melvin. "Three African poets," African Forum, I, 3 (Winter 1966), 121-123. [Nwanodi, Peters, Awoonor-Williams]

AFRICAN PERSONALITY

158. Beier, Ulli. "In search of an African personality," Twentieth Century, CLXV, 986 (April 1959), 343-349.

159. Esedebe, Peter Olisanwuche. "What is meant by African personality?" Insight, 7 (n.d.), 23-25.

160. July, Robert W. "African literature and the African personality," Black Orpheus, 14 (1964), 33-45.

161. Kaggwa, Norbert. "Monument to rebirth," Transition, II, 6-7 (1962), 41-42.

162. Shelton, Austin J. "The cyclic principal of African personality," Presence Africaine, Eng. ed., XVII, 45 (1963), 145-150.


ENGLISH LANGUAGE

163. Achebe, Chinua. "English and the African writer," Transition, IV, 18 (1965), 27-30.

164. Ekpenyong, J.O. "The use of English in Nigeria," Commonwealth literature, John Press, ed. London: Heinemann, 1965, p.144-150.

165. "Getting through to the South African," TLS, 10 August 1962, p.572.

166. Johnson, Willard. "African-speaking Africa? lesson from the Cameroon," African Forum, I, 2 (Fall 1965), 65-77.

167. Mphahlele, Ezekiel. "The language of African literature," Language and learning, 9 (n.d.), 298-305.

168. Okwu, Edward C. "A language of expression for Nigerian literature," Nigeria Magazine, 91 (1966), 289-292.

169. Povey, John. "The threatened language," New African, IV, 10 (December 1965), 242-243.

170. Warner, Alan. "A new English in Africa?" Review of English Literature, IV, 2 (April 1963), 45-54.


LITERARY CRITICISM

171. Achebe, Chinua. "Where angels fear to tread," Nigeria Magazine, 75 (1962), 61-62.

172. Lagneau-Kesteloot, L. "Problems of the literary critic in
     Africa," Abbia, 8 (February-March 1965), 29-44

173. Wake, Clive H. "African literary criticism," Comparative
     Literature Studies, I (1964), 197-205.

174. Wright, Edgar. "African literature I: problems of criticism,"
     J. of Commonwealth Literature, 2 (December 1966), 103-112.


## LITTLE MAGAZINES

175. Povey, John. "The little magazines soldier on," New African,
     V, 1 (January 1966), 16.

176. Segal, Philip. "Taking stock with The Classic," Contrast, II
     3 (1963-64), 5-10.


## MARKET LITERATURE

177. Beier, Ulli. "Public opinion on lovers," Black Orpheus, 14
     (1964), 4-16.

178. Nwoga, Donatus I. "Onitsha market literature," Transition,
     IV, 19 (1965), 26-33.

179. Schmidt, Nancy J. "Nigeria: fiction for the average man,"
     Africa Report, X, 8 (August 1965), 39-41.

180. Young, Peter. "A note from Onitsha," Bulletin of the Association
     for African Literature in English, 4 (1966), 37-40.


## MBARI

181. Hendrickse, Begum. "The Mbari story," African Forum, I, 1
     (Summer 1965), 109-110.

182. Mphahlele, Ezekiel. "Mbari - first anniversary," Africa
     Report, VII, 11 (December 1962), 17.

183. Ulansky, Gene. "Mbari - the missing link," Phylon, XXVI, 3
     (Fall 1965), 247-254.

184. Williams, Denis. "The Mbari publications," Nigeria Magazine, 75
     (1962), 70.

NEGRITUDE

185. Bastide, Roger. "Variations on negritude," Presence Africaine,
     Eng. ed., VIII, 36 (1961), 83-91.

186. Blair, Dorothy S. "Negritude: I," Contrast, I, 2 (1961),
     38-48; "Negritude: II," Contrast, I, 3 (1961), 38-49.

187. --. "Whither negritude?" Classic, II, 2 (1966), 5-10.

188. Feuser, Willfried. "Negritude - the third phase," New African,
     V, 3 (April 1966), 63-64.

189. Furay, Michael. "Negritude - a romantic myth?" New Republic,
     CXLV, 1 (1966), 32-35.

190. --. "Negritude and the Dakar Festival," Bulletin of the
     Association for African Literature in English, 4 (1966), 1-12.

191. Irele, Abiola. "Negritude or black cultural nationalism?"
     J. of Modern African Studies, III, 3 (October 1965), 321-348.

192. --. "Negritude - literature and ideology," J. of Modern African
     Studies, III, 4 (December 1965), 499-526. Includes bibliography.

193. --. "In defence of negritude," Transition, III, 13 (1964), 9-11.

194. Jeanpierre, W.A. "'Negritude' - its development and significance,"
     Presence Africaine, Eng. ed., XI, 39 (1961), 32-49.

195. "Keeping it dark," TLS, 21 September 1962, p.702-703.

196. Kennedy, Ellen, and Paulette J. Trout. "The roots of negritude,"
     Africa Report, XI, 5 (May 1966), 61-62.

197. Melone, Thomas. "The theme of negritude and its literary problems,"
     Presence Africaine, Eng. ed., XX, 48 (1963), 166-181.

198. Mphahlele, Ezekiel. "The cult of negritude," Encounter, XVI, 3
     (March 1961), 50-52.

199. Rive, Richard. "Images of drums and tom-toms," Contrast, III,
     1 (1964), 48-54.

200. Shelton, Austin J. "The black mystique: reactionary extremes
     in 'negritude'," African Affairs, 63 (April 1964), 115-128.

201. Senghor, Leopold Sedar. "Negritude and the concept of universal civilization," Presence Africaine, Eng. ed., XVIII, 46 (1963), 9-13.

202. --. "On Negrohood: psychology of the African Negro," Diogenes, 37 (Spring 1962), 1-15.

203. Simon, Erica. "Negritude and cultural problems of contemporary Africa," Presence Africaine, Eng. ed., XIX, 47 (1963), 122-146.

204. Thomas, L.V. "Senghor and negritude," Presence Africaine, Eng. ed., XXVI, 54 (1965), 102-132.

205. "Twilight of a dark myth," TLS, 16 September 1965, p.805-806.

CONFERENCES

Berlin. Working Congress on African Poetry. Berlin Festival. October 1964.

206. Mphahlele, Ezekiel. "Africa at the Berlin Festival," Africa and the World (December 1964), 43-45.

207. Rive, Richard. "African poets in Berlin," Contrast, III, 3 (1965), 66-69.

Dakar-Fourah Bay Conference. March-April 1963.

208. Moore, Gerald, and Donald Stuart. "African literature, French and English," Makerere J., 8 (1963), 29-34.

209. Mphahlele, Ezekiel. "African literature and universities," Transition, III, 10 (1963), 16-18.

210. "Who reads it?" TLS, 16 September 1965, p.801.

Dakar. First World Festival of Negro Arts. April 1966.

211. New African, V, 3 (April 1966). Dakar Festival supplement.

212. Nzekwu, Onuora. "Nigeria, negritude and the World Festival of Negro Arts," Nigeria Magazine, 89 (1966), 80-94.

213. Povey, John. "Dakar, an African rendezvous," Africa Today,
     XIII, 5 (May 1966), 4-7.

214. --. "The first World Festival of the Negro Arts at Dakar,"
     J. of the New African Literature, 2 (Fall 1966), 24-30.

215. Senghor, Leopold Sedar. "The function and meaning of the first
     World Festival of Negro Arts," African Forum, I, 4
     (Spring 1966), 5-10.


Kampala. 11-16 June 1962. Conference of African Writers of
     English Expression.

216. "Africa's writers meet," West African Review, XXXII, 417
     (September 1962), 17-19.

217. Fonlon, Bernard. "African writers meet in Uganda," Abbia,
     1 (February 1963), 39-53.

218. --. "Report on the Kampala Conference," Presence Africaine,
     Eng. ed., XVII, 45 (1963), 130-144.

219. Modisane, Bloke. "African writers' summit," Transition, II
     5 (1962), 5-6.

220. Mphahlele, Ezekiel. "Press report, Conference of African Writers
     of English Expression," Makerere J., V, 2 (1962).

221. Nagenda, John. "Conference notebook," Transition, II, 5 (1962),
     8-9.

222. Rive, Richard. "No common factor," Contrast, II, 4 (1964),
     52-56.

223. Segal, Philip. "We sing of Africa," Contrast, II, 2 (1963),
     7-13.

224. "Transition Conference questionnaire" [Langston Hughes, Arthur
     Drayton, Bloke Modisane, Robie Macauley, Bernard Fonlon,
     Christopher Okigbo], Transition, II, 5 (1962), 11-12.


London. Commonwealth Arts Festival. September 1965.

225. J.A.M. "Clark and Soyinka at the Commonwealth Arts Festival,"
     New African, IV, 8 (October 1965), 195.

226.  New African, IV, 7 (September 1965).  Commonwealth Arts Festival
      supplement.


      Paris.  First International Conference of Negro Writers and Artists.
      19-22 September 1956.

227.  Jahn, Janheinz.  "World congress of black writers,"  Black
      Orpheus, 1 (1957), 39-46.

228.  Presence Africaine, Eng. ed., 8-10 (1956).  Special number.


      Rome.  Second International Congress of Negro Writers and Artists.
      26 March - 1 April 1959.

229.  Presence Africaine,  Eng. ed., XXIV-XXV, 42-43 (1959).  Special
      number.


      Salisbury, So. Rhodesia.  November 1958.

230.  Moore, Gerald.  "African writing seen from Salisbury,"  Presence
      Africaine, Eng. ed., III, 31 (1960), 87-94.

Anthologies

231. ADEMOLA, FRANCES, ed.
Reflections: Nigerian prose and verse.
Lagos: African Universities Press, 1962. 123p.
Pref. Ezekiel Mphahlele.
Lagos: African Universities Press, 1965. 119p.
Foreword Dr. Nnamdi Azikiwe.

Rev: TLS, 20 September 1963, p.709.
M. Banham, Books Abroad, XXXVIII, 2 (Spring 1964),
210-211.

232. BANHAM, MARTIN, ed.
Nigerian student verse, 1959; a selection of verse written
by students of the University College, Ibadan, and first
published in "The Horn."
Ibadan: Ibadan University Press, 1960. 33p.

233. BASSIR, OLUMBE, ed.
An anthology of West African verse.
Ibadan: Ibadan University Press, 1957. xii, 68p.

Rev: Akanji, Black Orpheus, 3 (1958), 58-59.

234. BEIER, ULLI, ed.
Black Orpheus: an anthology of new African and Afro-American
stories.
Ikeja: Longmans of Nigeria, 1964. 156p.
New York: McGraw-Hill, 1965. 156p.

Rev: TLS, 29 April 1965, p.323.
Henry Swanzy, New African, IV, 5 (July 1965), 112.

235. COOK, DAVID, ed.
Origin East Africa: a Makerere anthology.
London: Heinemann (African Writers Series, no.15),
1965. xii, 188p.

Rev: TLS, 29 April 1965, p.323.
M. Blumberg, New African, IV, 4 (June 1965), 90-91.
Michael Ligny, Presence Africaine, Eng. ed., XXVIII,
55 (1965), 219-221.

236. DENNY, NEVILLE, ed.
     Pan African short stories;  an anthology for schools.
          London:  Nelson, 1965.  xvi, 223p. Illus. Louis
          Mwaniki.


237. DRACHLER, JACOB, ed.
     African heritage;  intimate views of the black Africans
          from life, lore, and literature.  Pref. Melville J.
     Herskovits.
          New York:  Crowell-Collier, 1963. 286p.
          London:  Crowell-Macmillan, 1963. 286p.
          New York:  Collier Books, 1964. 286p.
          London:  Crowell-Macmillan, 1964.  286p.


238. EDWARDS, PAUL, ed.
     Modern African narrative.
          London:  Nelson, 1966. 196p.

     Rev:  Peter Young,  Bulletin of the Association for African
          Literature in English, 4 (1966), 43-44.


     Through African eyes.
          Cambridge [Eng.] University Press, 1966. 2v.


     West African narrative;  an anthology for schools.
          London:  Nelson, 1963.  iv, 252p.  Illus. Caroline
          Sassoon and John Cottrell.


239. HUGHES, LANGSTON, ed.
     An African treasury;  articles, essays, stories, poems by
          black Africans.
               New York:  Crown, 1960.  xiv, 207p.
               London:  Gollancz, 1961.  xiv, 207p.
               New York:  Pyramid Books (R606), 1961.

     Rev:  Bernard Fonlon,  Presence Africaine, Eng. ed., VI-VII,
               34-35 (1960), 239-240.
          Tom Hopkinson,  Observer, 17 September 1961, p.28.
          E. Mphahlele,  Black Orpheus, 9 (1961), 67-68.


     Poems from black Africa.
          Bloomington:  Indiana University Press, 1963.  158p.

Bloomington: Indiana University Press (Midland Books Poetry Paperbacks), 1966. 158p.

Rev: TLS, 2 August 1963, p.594.
Abiola Irele, Presence Africaine, Eng. ed., XXI, 49 (1964), 275-278.

240. KOMEY, ELLIS AYITEY, and EZEKIEL MPHAHLELE, eds.
Modern African stories.
London: Faber, 1964, 1966. 227p.

Rev: TLS, 12 November 1964, p.1016.
Bernice G. Duncan, Books Abroad, XXXIX, 3 (Summer 1965), 370.
Frank Hercules, African Forum, I, 2 (Fall 1965), 113-114.
O.R. Dathorne, Black Orpheus, 18 (1965), 60.
Michael Ligny, Presence Africaine, Eng. ed., XXVIII, 56 (1965), 163-170.
Gerald Moore, Transition, V, 23 (1965), 45-46.

241. MOORE, GERALD, and ULLI BEIER, eds.
Modern poetry from Africa
Harmondsworth, Baltimore: Penguin (Penguin African Library, AP 7), 1963. 192p.

Rev: TLS, 16 August 1963, p.626.
Gerhard Friedrich, Books Abroad, XXXVIII, 2 (Spring 1964), 214.
Abiola Irele, Presence Africaine, Eng. ed., XXI, 49 (1964), 275-278.

242. MPHAHLELE, EZEKIEL, ed.
African writing today.
Harmondsworth, Baltimore: Penguin, 1967. 347p.

243. PRESENCE AFRICAINE, XXIX, 57 (1966), "New sum of poetry from the Negro world." ["African poetry of English expression," p.263-350.]

244. REED, JOHN, and CLIVE WAKE, eds.
     <u>A book of African verse.</u>
               London: Heinemann (African Writers Series, no.8),
               1964. viii, 119p.

     Rev: O.R. Dathorne, <u>Bulletin of the Association for</u>
               <u>African Literature in English,</u> 2 (n.d.), 27-28.
          <u>TLS</u>, 11 June 1964, p.501-502.
          M.M. Mahood, <u>East Africa Journal</u> (March 1965), 38.


245. RIDOUT, RONALD, and ELDRED JONES, eds.
     <u>Adjustments; an anthology of African and western writing.</u>
               London: Edward Arnold, 1966. iv, 164p.


246. RIVE, RICHARD, ed.
     <u>Modern African prose.</u>
               London: Heinemann (African Writers Series, no.9),
               1964. xv, 214p. Illus. Albert Adams.

     Rev: <u>TLS</u>, 1 April 1965, p.252.
          O.R. Dathorne, <u>Black Orpheus</u>, 17 (1965), 60.


     <u>Quartet; new voices from South Africa.</u> Intro. Alan Paton.
               New York: Crown, 1963. 223p.
               London: Heinemann (African Writers Series, no.14),
               1964. viii, 150p.

     Rev: Bernth Lindfors, <u>Books Abroad</u>, XXXIX, 2 (Spring 1965),
               240.
          Michael Ligny, <u>Presence Africaine</u>, Eng. ed., XXVIII,
               56 (1965), 178-179.


247. RUTHERFOORD, PEGGY, ed.
     <u>African voices; an anthology of native African writing.</u>
          Foreword Can Themba. Pref. Trevor Huddleston. [American
          edition of Darkness and light.]
               New York: Vanguard Press, 1958. 208p.

     Rev: Ezekiel Mphahlele, <u>Black Orpheus</u>, 6 (1959), 55.
          <u>TLS</u>, 18 October 1963, p.830.

Darkness and light;  an anthology of African writing.  Pref.
Trevor Huddleston.
London:  Faith Press, 1958, 1963.  208p.
Johannesburg:  Drum Publications, 1958.  208p.

Rev:  TLS,  6 March 1959, p.131.

248.  SWANZY, HENRY, ed.
Voices of Ghana;  literary contributions to the Ghana Broadcasting System, 1955-57.
Accra:  Ministry of Information and Broadcasting,
1958.  266p.

249.  TIBBLE, ANNE, ed.
African/English literature;  a short survey and anthology
of prose and poetry up to 1965.
London:  Peter Owen, 1965.  xvi.  304p.
New York:  October House, 1965.  xvi.  304p.

Rev:  Collingwood August,  New African, IV, 10 (December
1965), 230-231.
Angus Wilson,  Observer, 30 January 1966.

250.  WHITELEY, WILFRED H., ed.
A selection of African prose.  Foreword Chinua Achebe.
Oxford:  Oxford University Press (Oxford Library of
African Literature), 1964.  2v.

Rev:  TLS,  11 June 1964, p.501-502.

Authors

251.  ABBS, AKOSUA                          Ghana

> Ashanti boy. (novel)
> London: Collins, 1959. 256p.


252.  ABODERIN, S.F., 1928?-                Nigeria

> Anthologized in:
> Rutherfoord. African voices.


253.  ABRAHAMS, PETER, 1919-               South Africa

> Dark testament. (stories)
> London: G. Allen, 1942. 160p.


> Mine boy. (novel)
> London: D. Crisp, 1946. 183p.
> London: Faber, 1954. 252p.
> New York: Knopf, 1955. 252p.
> London: Heinemann (African Writers Series, no.6),
> 1963. 251p. Illus. Ruth Yudelowitz.


> A night of their own. (novel)
> London: Faber, 1965. 269p.
> New York: Knopf, 1965. 236p.

> Rev: R. Zuckerman, Books Abroad, XL, 1 (Winter 1966), 116.
> Wilfred Cartey, African Forum, I, 3 (Winter 1966),
> 115-121.


> The path of thunder. (novel)
> New York: Harper, 1948. 278p.
> London: Faber, 1952. 262p.


> Return to Goli. (essay)
> London: Faber, 1953. 224p.

Song of the city. (novel)
    London: D. Crisp, 1945. 180p.


Tell freedom; memories of Africa. (autobiography)
    London: Faber, 1954. 311p.
    New York: Knopf, 1954. 370p.


Wild conquest. (novel)
    New York: Harper, 1950. 309p.
    London: Faber, 1951. 382p.
    London: Penguin, 1966. 252p.


A wreath for Udomo. (novel)
    London: Faber, 1956. 309p.
    New York: Knopf, 1956. 356p.

Rev: Akanji, Black Orpheus, 4 (1958), 56-58.
    M.J.C. Echeruo, African Writer, I, 1 (August 1962),
    16-17.


Anthologized in:
    Hughes. An African treasury.
    --. Poems from black Africa.
    Rive. Modern African prose.
    Rutherfoord. African voices.
    Tibble. African/English literature.


254. ABRUQUAH, JOSEPH WILFRED        Ghana

The catechist. (novel)
    London: G. Allen & Unwin, 1965. 202p. Foreword
    Elspeth Huxley.

Rev: Danielle C. Cooper, Books Abroad, XL, 2 (Spring 1966),
    228.


255. ACHEBE, CHINUA, 1930- Nigeria

Arrow of God. (novel)
    London: Heinemann, 1964. 304p.
    London: Heinemann (African Writers Series, no.16),
    1965. 287p.

Rev:   <u>TLS</u>, 26 March 1964, p.249.
     John Ginger, <u>Black Orpheus</u>, 16 (1964), 59-60.
     Abiola Irele, <u>Presence Africaine</u>, Eng. ed., XXIV,
       52 (1964), 234-237.
     Gerald Moore, <u>Transition</u>, IV, 14 (1964), 52.
     Saunders Redding, <u>African Forum</u>, I, 1 (Summer 1965),
       142-143.
     Eldred Jones, <u>J. of Commonwealth Literature</u>, 1
       (September 1965), 176-178.


<u>Chike and the river</u>. (juvenilia)
     Cambridge [Eng.] University Press, 1966. 63p. Illus.
     Prue Theobalds.


<u>A man of the people</u>. (novel)
     London: Heinemann, 1966. 166p.
     New York: John Day, 1966. 166p.

Rev:   D.A.N. Jones, <u>New Statesman</u>, 28 January 1966, p.132-133.
     Angus Wilson, <u>Observer</u>, 30 January 1966.
     Robert Green, <u>Nation</u>, CCII, 16 (18 April 1966), 465-466.
     H.L.B. Moody, <u>Nigeria Magazine</u>, 89 (1966), 129-131.
     Joseph Okpaku, <u>J. of the New African Literature</u>, 2
      (Fall 1966), 76-80.


<u>No longer at ease</u>. (novel)
     London: Heinemann, 1960. 170p.
     New York: McDowell, Obolensky, 1960. 170p.
     London: Heinemann (African Writers Series, no.3),
      1963. 169p.

Rev:   <u>TLS</u>, 14 October 1960, p.666.
     Omidiji Aragbabalu, <u>Black Orpheus</u>, 8 (1960), 51-52.


<u>The sacrificial egg, and other short stories</u>.
     Onitsha: Etudo Ltd., 1962. iii, 32p. Illus. R. Ndefo.


<u>Things fall apart</u>. (novel)
     London: Heinemann, 1958. 185p.
     New York: McDowell, Obolensky, 1959. 215p.
     London: Heinemann (African Writers Series, no.1),
      1962. 187p. Illus. Dennis Carabine.

Rev:  Diana Speed, Black Orpheus, 5 (1959), 52.
        G. Adali Mortty, Black Orpheus, 6 (1959), 48-50
        Eldred Jones, Review of English Literature, V, 4
        (October 1964), 39-43.

"Chike's school days," (story) Rotarian (April 1960),
19-20.

"Uncle Ben's choice," (story) Black Orpheus, 19 (1966),
45-47.

"The voter," (story) Black Orpheus, 17 (1965), 4-7.


Anthologized in:
      Ademola. Reflections.
      Denny. Pan African short stories.
      Edwards. West African narrative.
      Komey. Modern African stories.
      Mphahlele. African writing today.
      Ridout. Adjustments.
      Rive. Modern African prose.
      Tibble. African/English literature.
      Whiteley. A selection of African prose.


Criticism:
      Abiola Irele. "The tragic conflict in Achebe's
        novels," Black Orpheus, 17 (1965), 24-32.

      Austin Shelton. "The offended chi in Achebe's
        novels," Transition, III, 13 (1964), 36-37.


256.  ADALI-MORTTI, GEORMBEEYI, 1916-        Ghana

      Anthologized in:
        Hughes. Poems from black Africa.
        Swanzy. Voices of Ghana.


257.  ADDO, JOYCE, 1932-            Ghana

      Anthologized in:
        Swanzy. Voices of Ghana.

258.  ADEBAYO, YEJIDE                          Nigeria

    Three plays.
        Lagos:  Nigerian Printing and Publishing Co., 1957.  55p.


259.  ADEYEMO, G.A.                            Nigeria

    Anthologized in:
        Banham.  Nigerian student verse.


260.  AGBADJA, ADOLPH KWESI AFORDOANYI, 1928- Ghana

    Anthologized in:
        Swanzy.  Voices of Ghana.


261.  AIDOO, CHRISTINA AMA ATA, 1942-          Ghana

    The dilemma of a ghost.  (drama)
        Accra:  Longmans, 1965.  50p.

    Rev:  Eldred Jones, Bulletin of the Association for African
          Literature in English, 2 (n.d.), 33-34.
          C.J. Rea, African Forum, I, 1 (Summer 1965), 111-113.
          Bernth Lindfors, Books Abroad, XL, 3 (Summer 1966),
          358-359.

    "Certain winds from the south," (story) Black Orpheus, 20.

    "A gift from somewhere," (story) J. of the New African
    Literature, 2 (Fall 1966), 36-44.

    "The late bud," (story) Okyeame, II, 2 (June 1965), 29-36.

    "The message," (story) Okyeame, III, 1 (December 1966),
    33-40.


    Anthologized in:
        Beier.  Black Orpheus anthology.
        Denny.  Pan African short stories.
        Komey.  Modern African stories.
        Mphahlele.  African writing today.
        Presence Africaine, no. 57.

262. AIG-IMOUKHUEDE, FRANK ABIODUN, 1935-    Nigeria

Anthologized in:
 Banham. Nigerian student verse.
 Hughes. Poems from black Africa.
 Moore. Modern poetry from Africa.

263. AIYEGBUSI, TUNDE      Nigeria

Anthologized in:
 Cook. Origin East Africa.

264. AJAO, ADEROGBA, 1930-    Nigeria

On the tiger's back. (autobiography)
 London: G. Allen & Unwin, 1962. 149p.
 Cleveland: World, 1962. 149p.

Rev: TLS, 10 August 1962, p.574.
 Robert Vlach, Books Abroad, XXXVII, 1 (Winter 1963), 103.

265. AJOSE, AUDREY      Nigeria

Yomi's adventures. (juvenilia)
 Cambridge ⌈Eng.⌉ University Press, 1964. 90p. Illus.
 Mick Pilcher.

266. AKINSEMOYIN, KUNLE    Nigeria

Stories at sundown. (juvenilia)
 London: Harrap, 1965. 71p.

Twilight and the tortoise. (juvenilia)
 Lagos: African Universities Press (African Reader's
 Library, no.3), 1963. 80p. Illus. Stephen Erhabor.

Twilight tales. (juvenilia)
 Lagos: African Universities Press (African Reader's
 Library, no.10), 1965. 79p. Illus. Prue Theobalds.

Anthologized in:
    Bassir. An anthology of West African verse

267. AKOBO, B.                             Nigeria

Anthologized in:
    Banham. Nigerian student verse

268. AKPAN, NTIEYONG UDO              Nigeria

Ini Abasi and the sacred ram. (juvenilia)
    London: Longmans, 1966. 25p.

The wooden gong. (novel)
    London: Longmans, 1965. 117p.

Rev: Edgar Wright, Transition, V, 25 (1966), 52-54.

269. AKPOYOWARE, MAC                Nigeria

Anthologized in:
    Banham. Nigerian student verse.

270. ALUKO, TIMOTHY MOFOLORUNSO, 1918-     Nigeria

Kinsman and foreman. (novel)
    London: Heinemann, 1966.
    London: Heinemann (African Writers Series, no.32), 1967.

One man, one matchet. (novel)
    London: Heinemann (African Writers Series, no.11),
        1964. 196p.

Rev: TLS, 12 November 1964, p.1016.
    Alfred Hutchinson, New African, IV, 5 (July 1965), 114.
    I.N.C. Aniebo, Nigeria Magazine, 85 (1965), 141-144.
    Edgar Wright, Transition, V, 25 (1966), 52-54.
    Geoffrey Caston, African Forum, I, 3 (Winter 1966), 124-1
    Nunasu Amosu, Black Orpheus, 19 (1966), 61.

One man, one wife. (novel)
      Lagos: Nigerian Printing and Publishing Co., 1959. 200p.
      London: Heinemann (African Writers Series, no.30), 1967.

Rev: Ulli Beier, Black Orpheus, 6 (1959), 52-54.

271. AMADI, ELECHI, 1934-               Nigeria

The concubine. (novel)
      London: Heinemann, 1966. 279p.
      London: Heinemann (African Writers Series, no.25), 1966.

Rev: TLS, 7 April 1966, p.281.
     D. Thompson, New African, V, 3 (April 1966), 73.

272. ANIEBO, I.N.C.               Nigeria

"Dilemma," (story) Nigeria Magazine, 79 (1963), 284-287.

"Four dimensions," (story) Black Orpheus, 18 (1965), 9-16.

"Mirage," (story) Nigeria Magazine, 88 (1966), 50-54.

"The release," (story) Spear (October 1963), 31-33.

"The symbols," (story) Nigeria Magazine, 91 (December 1966),
   294-296.

273. ANNAN, KWABENA             Ghana

Anthologized in:
      Komey. Modern African Stories.

274. ARCHIBALD-AIKINS, SAMUEL E., 1932-    Ghana

Anthologized in:
      Swanzy. Voices of Ghana.

275. ARKHURST, FREDERICK S.         Ghana

Anthologized in:
      Hughes. An African treasury.

276. ARMAH, AYI KWEI                                    Ghana

"Asemka," (story) Okyeame, III, 1 (December 1966), 28-32.

"Contact," (story) New African, IV, 10 (December 1965), 244-246.


277. ASALACHE, KHADAMBI                                 Kenya

A calabash of life. (novel)
        London: Longmans, 1967.


278. AWOONOR-WILLIAMS, GEORGE, 1935-                    Ghana

Rediscovery, and other poems.
        Ibadan: Mbari, 1964. 36p.

Rev: Omidiji Aragbalu, Black Orpheus, 17 (1965), 61-62.


"The funeral," (story) Okyeame, II, 2 (June 1965), 22.

"Just to buy corn," (story) Okyeame, II, 1 (1964), 22-30.


Anthologized in:
        Moore. Modern poetry from Africa.
        Mphahlele. African writing today.
        Presence Africaine, no. 57.
        Reed. A book of African verse.
        Tibble. African/English literature.


279. BABALOLA, ADEBOYE                                  Nigeria

Anthologized in:
        Bassir. An anthology of West African verse.
        Reed. A book of African verse.


280. BEDWEI, ATO                                        Ghana

Anthologized in:
        Komey. Modern African stories.

281.  BERENG, MASUPHA, 1928-                    Basutoland

    Anthologized in:
        Rutherfoord.  African voices.


282.  BLAY, J. BENIBENGOR                       Ghana

    Dr. Bengia wants a wife.  (story)
        London:  Blackheath Press, 1953.  23p.


    Ghana sings.  (verse)
        Accra:  Waterville Publishing House, 1965.  78p.


    Here and there stories.
        Accra:  Bureau of Ghana Languages, 1959.  24p.


    Stubborn girl.  (story)
        Accra:  Guinea Press, 1958.  22p.


    Thoughts of youth.  (novel)
        Aboso, Ghana:  Benibengor Book Agency, 1961.  130p.


    Anthologized in:
        Hughes.  An African treasury.

283.  BOETIE, DUGMORE                           South Africa

    "The last leg,"  (story)  Classic, I, 2 (1963), 25-31.

284.  BONDY, SABASTIAN SALAZAR                  Nigeria

    The suitcase; a plaything in one act.  Adapted for Theatre
      Express by Obotunde Ijimere.
        Oshogbo:  Theatre Express Sketches, 1966.  26p.

285. BREW, KWESI, 1928–                    Ghana

    Anthologized in:
        Hughes.  Poems from black Africa.
        Moore.  Modern poetry from Africa.
        Mphahlele.  African writing today.
        Reed.  A book of African verse.
        Swanzy.  Voices of Ghana.
        Tibble.  African/English literature.


286. BROWN, C. ENITAN, 1909–               Nigeria

    Anthologized in:
        Rutherfoord.  African voices


287. BRUTUS, DENNIS                        S. Rhodesia

    Sirens, knuckles and boots.  (verse)
        Ibadan:  Mbari, 1963.

    Rev:  Ulli Beier, Black Orpheus, 12 (1963), 46–50.
          Daniel Abasiekong,  Transition, V, 23 (1965), 45–48.

    Anthologized in:
        Mphahlele.  African writing today.
        Presence Africaine, no. 57
        Tibble.  African/English literature.


288. BUAHIN, PETER KWAME, 1931–            Ghana

    Anthologized in:
        Komey.  Modern African stories.
        Swanzy.  Voices of Ghana.


289. CHACHA, TOM                           Tanganyika

    Anthologized in:
        Cook.  Origin East Africa.
        Denny.  Pan African short stories.

90. CHIJIOKE, MARK                    Nigeria

    Anthologized in:
        Bassir. An anthology of West African verse.

91. CITASHE, I.W.W.              South Africa

    Anthologized in:
        Hughes. An African treasury.

92. CLARK, JOHN PEPPER, 1935-        Nigeria

    America, their America. (autobiography)
        London: Deutsch, 1964. 221p.

    Rev: TLS, 24 September 1964, p.3265.
        M. Banham, Books Abroad, XXXIX, 2 (Spring 1965), 328.
        William Walsh, J. of Commonwealth Literature, 1 (September
          1965), 169-172.
        I.N.C. Aniebo, Nigeria Magazine, 85 (1965), 136-138.
        O.R. Dathorne, Black Orpheus, 18 (1965), 60-61.
        Wole Soyinka, Ibadan, 22 (June 1966), 59-61.

    Ozidi. (drama)
        London: Oxford University Press (Three Crowns Book),
          1966. 121p.

    Poems.
        Ibadan: Mbari, 1962. 51p. Illus. Susanne Wenger.

    Rev: Ulli Beier, Black Orpheus, 12 (1963), 46-50.
        M. Banham, Books Abroad, XXXVIII, 1 (Winter 1964), 92.

    A reed in the tide. (verse)
        London: Longmans (Forum Series), 1965. viii, 40p.

    Rev: Bernice Duncan, Books Abroad, XL, 3 (Summer 1966), 361.
        Taban lo Liyong, African Forum, II, 1 (Summer 1966),
          110-113.

Song of a goat. (drama)
Ibadan: Mbari, 1961. 43p.


Three plays: Song of a goat; The masquerade; The raft.
London: Oxford University Press (Three Crowns Book)
1964. 134p.

Rev: TLS, 13 August 1964, p.728.
Robert Fitzgerald, African Forum, I, 1 (Summer 1965),
143-145.
Geoffrey Hill, J. of Commonwealth Literature, 1
(September 1965), 172-174.
Charles Larson, Africa Report, XI, 8 (November 1966),
57-58.
Martin Esslin, Black Orpheus, 19 (1966), 33-39.


"A stop in the night," (story) Black Orpheus, 16 (1964), 35-37.


Anthologized in:
Ademola. Reflections.
Hughes. Poems from black Africa.
Moore. Modern Poetry from Africa.
Presence Africaine, no. 57.
Reed. A book of African verse.
Tibble. African/English literature.


Criticism:
Frances Ademola. "J.P. Clark and his audience," African
Forum, I, 2 (Fall 1965), 84-85.
Sunday O. Anozie. "Two Nigerian poets," African Writer,
I, 1 (August 1962), 3-4. [Osadebay and Clark]
Anthony Astrachan. "Like goats to the slaughter," Black
Orpheus, 16 (1964), 21-24.
Barry Reckord. "Notes on two Nigerian playwrights,"
New African, IV, 7 (September 1965), 171. [Clark and
Soyinka]


293. CLARKE, PETER, 1929-                    South Africa

Anthologized in:
Hughes. An African treasury.
--. Poems from black Africa.
Rive. Modern African prose.

294. COLE, ROBERT WELLESLEY, 1907-          Sierra Leone

      Kossoh town boy. (autobiography)
              Cambridge [Eng.] University Press, 1960.  190p.
              Illus. Felix Cobbson.

      Rev: TLS, 30 September 1960, p.622.
           Sangodare Akanji, Black Orpheus, 9 (1961), 66.


295. CONTON, WILLIAM FARQUHAR, 1925-          Gambia

      The African. (novel)
              London: Heinemann, 1960.  244p.
              Boston: Little, Brown, 1960.  244p.
              New York: New American Library (Signet D1906), 1961.
              London: Heinemann (African Writers Series, no.12),
                1964.  213p.

      Rev: Erisa Kironde, Black Orpheus, 10 (1962), 67-68.


      Anthologized in:
              Denny.  Pan African short stories.
              Edwards.  West African narrative.
              Komey.  Modern African stories.
              Ridout.  Adjustments.
              Rive.  Modern African prose.
              Tibble.  African/English literature.


296. CUDJOE, SETH D., 1910-          Ghana

      Anthologized in:
              Bassir.  An anthology of West African verse.
              Reed.  A book of African verse.
              Swanzy.  Voices of Ghana.


297. DADSON, I.B., 1920-          Ghana

      Anthologized in:
              Swanzy.  Voices of Ghana.

298. DE GRAFT, JOE C.                              Ghana

    Sons and daughters. (drama)
        London:  Oxford University Press (Three Crowns Book),
          1964.  53p.

    Rev:  TLS, 13 August 1964, p.728.
        Bernth Lindfors,  Books Abroad, XXXIX 3 (Summer 1965),
          364.
        Jo Cameron,  Black Orpheus, 19 (1966), 59-60.

    "Visitor from the past," (drama) Okyeame, II, 2 (June 1965),
    59-73.

299. DEI-ANANG, MICHAEL FRANCES, 1909-        Ghana

    Africa speaks; a collection of original verse with an
    introduction of "Poetry in Africa."
        Accra:  Guinea Press, 1959.  99p.

    Cocoa comes to Mampong. (drama)
        Cape Coast:  Methodist Book Depot, 1949.  47p.

    Ghana glory;  poems on Ghana and Ghanaian life, by Michael
    Dei-Anang and Yaw Warren.
        London:  Nelson, 1965.  69p.  Foreword Kwame Nkrumah.

    Ghana semi-tones. (verse)
        Accra:  Presbyterian Book Depot, 1962. 28p.

    Okomfo Anokye's golden stool. (drama)
        Ilfracombe, Devonshire:  Stockwell, 1959.  54p.
        Accra:  Waterville Publishing House, 1963.  60p.

    Two faces of Africa. (verse)
        Accra:  Waterville Publishing House, 1965.

    Wayward lines from Africa. (verse)
        London:  Lutterworth, 1946.
        London:  United Society for Christian Literature, 1946.
          47p.

Anthologized in:
    Hughes. An African treasury.
    --. Poems from black Africa.

300. DEMPSTER, ROLAND TOMBEKAI,     -1965     Liberia

The mystic reformation of Gondolia. (verse)
    London: Dragon Press, 1953.

A song out of midnight. (verse)
    London: Dragon Press, 1959.

To Monrovia old and new. (verse)
    London: Dragon Press, 1958.

Anthologized in:
    Hughes. Poems from black Africa.

301. DERIMANU, A.B., 1918-     Ghana

Anthologized in:
    Swanzy. Voices of Ghana.

302. DIPOKO, MBELLA SONNE, 1936-     Cameroon

A few nights and days. (novel)
    London: Longmans, 1966. 183p.

Rev: TLS, 21 July 1966, p.629.
    Paul Theroux, Transition, VI, 27 (1966), 52-53.

"A few nights and days," (story) New African, V, 3 (April 1966), 54-56.

"The same horizons," (story) Presence Africaine, Eng. ed., XXVIII, 56 (1965), 101-122.

"Trapped in Lagos," (story) Presence Africaine, Eng. ed., XIII, 41 (1962), 79-89.

Anthologized in:
    Mphahlele. <u>African writing today</u>.
    <u>Presence Africaine</u>, no.57.

303.  DJOLETO, S.A.A., 1929-        Ghana

    Anthologized in:
        Swanzy. <u>Voices of Ghana</u>.

304.  DOVE-DANQUAH, MABEL        Ghana

    Anthologized in:
        Hughes. <u>An African treasury</u>.
        Whiteley. <u>A selection of African prose</u>.

305.  DUODU, M. CAMERON, 1937-        Ghana

    "The tax dodger," (story) <u>Okyeame</u>, I (January 1961),
    23-33.

    Anthologized in:
        Swanzy. <u>Voices of Ghana</u>.

306.  EASMON, R. SARIF        Sierra Leone

    <u>Dear parent and ogre</u>. (drama)
        London: Oxford University Press (Three Crowns Book),
        1964. 101p.

    Rev: Elow Gabonal, <u>Black Orpheus</u>, 11 (1962), 65-66.
        G. Moore, <u>East Africa Journal</u> (June 1965), 36-37.
        B. Lindfors, <u>Books Abroad</u>, XL, 1 (Winter 1966), 115-116.
        Jo Cameron, <u>Black Orpheus</u>, 19 (1966), 59-60.

    <u>The new patriots</u>. (drama)
        London: Longmans, 1965. 90p.

    Anthologized in:
        Komey. <u>Modern African stories</u>.
        Mphahlele. <u>African writing today</u>.
        Ridout. <u>Adjustments</u>.

307.  ECHERUO, MICHAEL J.C., 1937-          Nigeria

Anthologized in:
    Moore.  Modern poetry from Africa.
    Presence Africaine, no.57.
    Tibble.  African/English literature.

308.  EGBUNA, OBI B.                        Nigeria

The anthill.  (drama)
    London:  Oxford University Press (Three Crowns Book),
      1965.  60p.

Rev:  B. Lindfors,  Books Abroad, XL, 3 (Summer 1966), 360.

Wind versus polygamy.  (novel)
    London:  Faber, 1964.  128p.

Rev:  M. Macmillan,  J. of Commonwealth Literature, 1
      (September 1965), 174-175.
      O.R. Dathorne,  Black Orpheus, 17 (1965), 59.
      M.S. Dipoko,  Presence Africaine, Eng. ed., XXV, 53
      (1965), 275-276.

"Daughters of the sun,"  (story)  New African, V, 6 (July 1966),
    121-123.

"Divinity,"  (radio drama)  New African, IV, 6 (August 1965),
    135-136;  IV, 7 (September 1965), 174-175.

309.  EKWENSI, CYPRIAN, 1921-              Nigeria

An African night's entertainment;  a tale of vengeance.
    (juvenilia)
      Lagos:  African Universities Press (African Reader's
        Library, no.1), 1962.  96p.  Illus. Bruce Onobrakpeya.

Rev:  TLS, 20 September 1963, p.709.

Beautiful feathers.  (novel)
    London:  Hutchinson, 1963.  159p.

Rev:  TLS, 17 May 1963, p.353.
      M. Ligny,  Presence Africaine, Eng. ed., XXIII, 51 (1964),
      177-178.
      Austin Shelton,  Books Abroad, XXXIX, 1 (Winter 1965),
      34-36.

The boa suitor. (juvenilia)
    London: Nelson, 1966. viii, 56p. Illus. John Cottrell.


Burning grass. (novel)
    London: Heinemann (African Writers Series, no.2),
       1962. 150p.


The drummer boy. (juvenilia)
    Cambridge [Eng.] University Press, 1960. 87p.


The great elephant-bird. (juvenilia)
    London: Nelson, 1965. xii, 68p. Illus. Rosemary
    Tonks and John Cottrell.


Ikolo the wrestler, and other Ibo tales.
    London: Nelson, 1947.


Iska. (novel)
    London: Hutchinson, 1966. 222p.

Rev: TLS, 25 August 1966, p.757.


Jagua Nana. (novel)
    London: Hutchinson, 1961. 192p.
    London: Panther Books, 1963. 143p.

Rev: Ulli Beier, Black Orpheus, 10 (1961), 68.


The leopard's claw. (novel)
    London: Longmans, 1950. 90p.


Lokotown, and other stories.
    London: Heinemann (African Writers Series, no.19),
       1966. 152p.

Rev: Charles Larson, Africa Report, XI, 7 (October 1966),
    75-76.
    Nancy J. Schmidt. J. of the New African Literature, 2
    (Fall 1966), 71-72.

Passport of Mallam Ilia.  (juvenilia)
      Cambridge [Eng.] University Press, 1960.  80p.


People of the city.  (novel)
      London:  Dakers, 1954.  237p.
      London:  Heinemann (African Writers Series, no.5),
        1963.  156p.
      Evanston:  Northwestern University Press, 1967.  156p.

Rev:  Elizabeth Bevan,  Black Orpheus, 4 (1958), 53-55.


The rainmaker, and other stories.  (juvenilia)
      Lagos:  African Universities Press (African Reader's
        Library, no.6), 1965.  80p.  Illus.  Prue Theobalds.

Rev:  Nancy Schmidt,  J. of the New African Literature, 2
      (Fall 1966), 71-72.


Trouble in form six.  (juvenilia)
      Cambridge [Eng.] University Press, 1966.  78p.  Illus.
      Prue Theobalds.


When love whispers.  (story)
      Onitsha:  Tabansi Bookshop, 1947.  44p.


"Drums and voices,"  (story)  Black Orpheus, 7 (1960), 40-45.

"Night of freedom,"  (story)  New African, V, 3 (April 1966),
      51-54.


Anthologized in:
      Ademola.  Reflections.
      Beier.  Black Orpheus anthology.
      Denny.  Pan African short stories.
      Hughes.  An African treasury.
      Komey.  Modern African stories.
      Mphahlele.  African writing today.
      Rive.  Modern African prose.
      Rutherfoord.  African voices.
      Tibble.  African/English literature.
      Whiteley.  A selection of African prose.

Criticism:
John Povey. "Cyprian Ekwensi and beautiful feathers,"
Critique, VIII, 1 (Fall 1965), 63-69.
Austin Shelton. "'Rebushing' or ontological recession
to Africanism: Jagua's return to the village,"
Presence Africaine, Eng. ed., XVIII, 46 (1963), 49-58.

310. EKWERE, JOHN D.                         Nigeria

Anthologized in:
Ademola. Reflections
Banham. Nigerian student verse.

311. EPELLE, SAM                             Nigeria

Anthologized in:
Reed. A book of African verse.

312. ESAN, YETUNDE                           Nigeria

Anthologized in:
Banham. Nigerian student verse.

313. EYAKUZE, VALENTINE                      Tanzania

Anthologized in:
Cook. Origin East Africa.

314. FALETI, ADEBAYO                         Nigeria

Anthologized in:
Hughes. Poems from black Africa.

315. GABRE-MEHDIN, TSEGAYE, 1935-            Ethiopia

Oda-oak oracle. (drama)
London: Oxford University Press (Three Crowns Book),
1965. 54p.

Anthologized in:
        Presence Africaine, no.57.


316.  GARDINER, ROBERT KWEKU ATTA, 1914-        Ghana

        Anthologized in:
                Swanzy.  Voices of Ghana.


317.  GATHERU, R. MUGO, 1925-                    Kenya

        Child of two worlds;  a Kikuyu's story.   Intro.  St. Clair
            Drake.  (autobiography)
                New York:  Praeger, 1964.  xiv, 216p.
                London:  Routledge and Kegan Paul, 1964.  xiv, 216p.
                London:  Heinemann (African Writers Series, no.20),
                    1966.  232p.

        Rev:  TLS,  19 March 1964, p.227.
              Mary Lystad,  Africa Report, X, 9 (October 1965), 61-62.


318.  GATUIRIA, JOSEPH                           Kenya

        Anthologized in:
                Cook.  Origin East Africa.
                Reed.  A book of African verse.


319.  GEORGE, CRISPIN                            Sierra Leone

        Precious gems unearthed.  (verse)
                1956.


        Anthologized in:
                Bassir.  An anthology of West African verse.


320.  GHARTEY, JOSEPH, 1911-                     Ghana

        Anthologized in:
                Swanzy.  Voices of Ghana.

321.  GICARU, MUGA                          Kenya

Land of sunshine:  scenes of life in Kenya before Mau Mau.
      (semi-autobiography)
            London:  Lawrence and Wishart, 1958.  175p.  Intro.
            Trevor Huddleston.


322.  GICOGO, GABRIEL                        Kenya

Anthologized in:
      Cook.  Origin East Africa.


323.  HAGAN, G.R., 1927-                      Ghana

Anthologized in:
      Swanzy.  Voices of Ghana.


324.  HALL, BARBARA, ed.                      Zambia

Tell me, Josephine.  (letters to the Central African Mail)
            London:  Deutsch, 1964.  142p.
            New York:  Simon and Schuster, 1964.  142p.  Foreword
            Kenneth Kaunda.

      Rev:  Bernice G. Duncan, Books Abroad, XXXIX, 1 (Winter 1965),
            112.
            W. Payne, Africa Report, X, 2 (February 1965), 57-58.


325.  HEAD, BESSIE                           S. Africa

"The green tree," (story) Transition, IV, 16 (1964), 33.

"Looking for a rain-god," (story) New African, V, 3 (April
      1966), 65.


326.  HENRIES, A. DORIS BANKS                 Liberia

Anthologized in:
      Presence Africaine, no.57.

327. HENSHAW, JAMES ENE, 1924-                    Nigeria

Children of the goddess, and other plays. [Includes Companion
for a chief; Magic in the blood]
London: University of London Press, 1964. 128p.


The jewels of the shrine.
Performed All-Nigeria Festival of the Arts, Lagos, 1952.


Medicine for love; a comedy in three acts.
London: University of London Press, 1964. 108p.


This is our chance. (drama)
London: University of London Press, 1956. 95p.


Criticism:
Geoffrey Axworthy. West African Journal of Education,
IX, 2 (June 1965), 103-105.


328. HIGO, AIG                                    Nigeria

Anthologized in:
Banham. Nigerian student verse.
Presence Africaine, no.57.
Reed. A book of African verse.


329. HIHETAH, ROBERT KOFI                         Ghana

"Neighbours," (story) Okyeame, II, 2 (June 1965), 37-41.

"Throwing stones at lizards," (story) Okyeame, II, 1 (1964),
31-33.


330. HOH, ISRAEL KAFU, 1912-                      Ghana

Anthologized in:
Swanzy. Voices of Ghana.

331. HOKORORO, ANTHONY M.

> Anthologized in:
> Cook. Origin East Africa.


332. HORATIO-JONES, EDWARD BABATUNDE BANKOLE, 1935-          Nigeria

> The mockers. (novel)
> Switzerland: Artemis Verlag, 1963.
>
> (One chapter of The mockers appeared in Black Orpheus, 10
> (1961), 11-21.)


333. HUTCHINSON, ALFRED, 1924-                S. Africa

> The rain killers. (drama)
> London: University of London Press, 1964. 80p.
>
> Rev: B. Lindfors, Books Abroad, XL, 3 (Summer 1966), 361.
>
>
> Road to Ghana. (autobiography)
> New York: John Day, 1960. 190p.
> London: Gollancz, 1960. 190p.
>
>
> "Fusane's trial," (radio drama) New African, IV, 4
> (June 1965), 83-84.
>
>
> Anthologized in:
> Komey. Modern African stories.
> Rive. Modern African prose.
> Tibble. African/English literature.


334. IDAN, L.K., 1921-                     Ghana

> Anthologized in:
> Swanzy. Voices of Ghana.

335. IJIMERE, OBOTUNDE, 1930-                    Nigeria

The fall. (drama)
      Oshogbo: Theatre Express Sketches, 1966.


The imprisonment of Obatala, and other plays. English
   adaptation by Ulli Beier.
      London: Heinemann (African Writers Series, no.18),
      1966. 109p.

Rev: Charles R. Larson, Africa Report, XI, 8 (November 1966),
     57-58.


336. IKE, VINCENT CHUKWUEMEKA, 1931-             Nigeria

Toads for supper. (novel)
      London: Harvill Press, 1965. 192p.
      London: Collins (Fontana Books), 1966.

Rev: TLS, 8 April 1965, p.269.
     Obi Egbuna, New African, IV, 10 (December 1965), 213.
     I.N.C. Aniebo, Nigeria Magazine, 86 (1965), 218-220.


"Waiting for his programme," (story) African Writer, I, 1
   (August 1962), 13-15.


337. IRELE, ABIOLA                              Nigeria

Anthologized in:
      Banham. Nigerian student verse.


338. JABAVU, NONI                               S. Africa

Drawn in colour; African contrasts. (autobiography)
      New York: St. Martin's Press, 1962. 208p.
      London: John Murray, 1960. 208p.


The ochre people; scenes from a South African life.
   (autobiography)
      New York: St. Martin's Press, 1963. 261p.
      London: John Murray, 1963. 261p.

Rev:   TLS, 17 May 1963, p.354.
       N. Bennett, Transition, V, 20 (1965), 20-21.

Anthologized in:
       Tibble.  African/English literature.


339.  JOHNSON, LEMUEL                         Sierra Leone

      "Amy's case (to Priscilla)," (story) J. of the New African
      Literature,  1 (Spring 1966), 64-68.


340.  JONES, ELDRED DUROSIMI                  Sierra Leone

      Anthologized in:
            Komey.  Modern African stories.


341.  JONES-QUARTEY, K.B.                     Ghana

      Anthologized in:
            Hughes.  Poems from black Africa.


342.  JORDAN, ARCHIBALD CAMPBELL, 1906-       S. Africa

      Anthologized in:
            Hughes.  Poems from black Africa.


343.  KACHINGWE, AUBREY, 1926-                Malawi

      No easy task.  (novel)
            London:  Heinemann, 1966.  233p.
            London:  Heinemann (African Writers Series, no.24), 1966.

      Rev:  TLS, 7 April 1966, p.281.
            D. Thompson,  New African, V, 3 (April 1966), 73.
            Howard S. Collins,  African Forum, II, 2 (Fall 1966),
               124-125.
            John Reed,  J. of Commonwealth Literature, 2 (December
               1966), 172-173.
            Lalage Bown,  Nigeria Magazine, 89 (1966), 127-129.
            Paul Theroux,  Transition, V, 25 (1966), 51.

344. KAGGWA, MICHAEL               Uganda

Anthologized in:
    Cook. Origin East Africa.


345. KAGWE, SOLOMON, 1939-         Kenya

Anthologized in:
    Cook. Origin East Africa.


346. KARIARA, JONATHAN, 1935-      Kenya

The green bean patch. Performed Uganda Drama Festival, 1960.

Anthologized in:
    Cook. Origin East Africa.
    Rive. Modern African prose.


347. KARIBO, MINJI                Nigeria

Anthologized in:
    Banham. Nigerian student verse.
    Reed. A book of African verse.


348. KARIENYE, M.

Anthologized in:
    Cook. Origin East Africa.


349. KARIUKI, JOSEPH E.          Kenya

Ode to Mzee. (verse)
    Nairobi: Chemchemi Cultural Center. 5p. Foreword Tom
        Mboya.

Anthologized in:
    Moore. Modern poetry from Africa.
    Mphahlele. African writing today.
    Presence Africaine, no.57.

350.   KARIUKI, JOSIAH MWANGI, 1929-          Kenya

Mau Mau detainee;  the account by a Kenya African of his
experiences in detention camps, 1953-1960.  (autobiography)
London:  Oxford University Press, 1963.  xxiii, 188p.
Foreword Margery Perham.

Rev:  TLS, 9 August 1963, p.602.
Ali Mazrui, Transition, III, 11 (1963), 23-28.
Bethwell A. Ogot, Makerere J., 9 (1964), 85-86.


351.   KAUNDA, KENNETH DAVID          Zambia

Zambia shall be free.  Foreword Stewart Gore Brown.  (autobiograp
London:  Heinemann (African Writers Series, no.4),
1962.  202p.
New York:  Praeger, 1963.  202p.

Rev:  J.G. Markham, J. of Modern African Studies, I, 3
(September 1963), 421-423.


352.   KAYIRA, LEGSON          Malawi

I will try.  (autobiography)
Garden City:  Doubleday, 1965.  251p.
London:  Longmans, 1965.  251p.

Rev:  M.H. Lystad, Africa Report, X, 9 (October 1965), 62.
Alfred Hutchinson, New African, V, 5 (June 1966), 115.
TLS, 14 July 1966, p.611.


353.   KHUNGA, CUTHBERT          Malawi

Anthologized in:
Cook.  Origin East Africa.


354.   KIBERA, LEONARD

Potent ash, by Leonard Kibera and Samuel Kahiga.  (stories)
Nairobi:  East African Publishing House  (Modern
African Library), 1967.

355. KIMENYE, BARBARA                          Uganda

Kalasanda. (stories)
        London:  Oxford University Press (Three Crowns Book),
        1965.  103p.  Illus. N. Kagwa.

Rev:  D. Thompson,  New African, V, 3 (April 1966), 73.
      B. Lindfors,  Books Abroad, XL, 4 (Autumn 1966), 489.
      Hebe Welbourn,  Transition, V, 24 (1966), 56.


Kalasanda revisited. (stories)
        London:  Oxford University Press (Three Crowns Book),
        1966.  110p.


"The pig,"  (story)  East Africa Journal  (September 1966),
51-55.


Anthologized in:
        Denny.  Pan African short stories.

356. KING, DELPHINE                          Sierra Leone

Dreams of twilight. (verse)
        Apapa:  Nigerian National Press, 1962.  71p.  Intro.
        Chinua Achebe.

357. KOKUNDA, VIOLET                         Uganda

Anthologized in:
        Cook.  Origin East Africa.

358. KOMEY, ELLIS AYITEY, 1927-               Ghana

Anthologized in:
        Hughes.  Poems from black Africa.
        Komey.  Modern African stories.
        Moore.  Modern poetry from Africa.
        Tibble.  African/English literature.

359.  KONADU, ASAME

      A woman in her prime.  (novel)
          London:  Heinemann (African Writers Series, no.40),
          1967.

360.  KUNENE, RAYMOND MAZISI, 1930-        S. Africa

      Anthologized in:
          Moore.  Modern poetry from Africa.
          Mphahlele.  African writing today.
          Presence Africaine, no.57.

      Criticism:
          Mofolo Bulane.  "Raymond Mazisi:  the new voice in
            African poetry,"  New African, V, 5 (June 1966),
            111-112.

361.  KURANKYI-TAYLOR, DOROTHY        Ghana

      Reflected thoughts.  (verse)
          Ilfracombe, Devonshire:  Stockwell, 1959.  39p.

362.  KYEI, KOJO GYINAYE, 1930-        Ghana

      Anthologized in:
          Hughes.  Poems from black Africa.

363.  LAGUMA, ALEX, 1925-        S. Africa

      And a threefold cord.  (novel)
          Berlin:  Seven Seas, 1964.  173p.

      Rev:  Wilfred Cartey, African Forum, I, 3 (Winter 1966),
          115-121.
          Bernth Lindfors, Books Abroad, XL, 1 (Winter 1966), 116.

      The stone country.  (novel)
          Berlin:  Seven Seas, 1967.

      A walk in the night.  (story)
          Ibadan:  Mbari, 1962.  90p.

Rev: M. Banham, Books Abroad, XXXVI, 4 (Autumn 1962), 458.
A. Astrachan, Black Orpheus, 14 (1964), 59.


"At the Portagees," (story) Black Orpheus, 11 (1962), 18-21.

"Blankets," (story) Black Orpheus, 15 (1964), 57-58.

"A glass of wine," (story) Black Orpheus, 7 (1960), 22-25.

"A matter of honour," (story) New African, IV, 7 (September 1965), 169-170.

"Slipper satin," (story) Black Orpheus, 8 (1960), 32-35.

"Tattoo marks and nails," (story) Black Orpheus, 14 (1964), 48-53.


Anthologized in:
    Denny. Pan African short stories.
    Komey. Modern African stories.
    Mphahlele. African writing today.
    Rive. Quartet.
    Tibble. African/English literature.


Criticism:
    B. Lindfors. "Form and technique in the novels of Richard Rive and Alex LaGuma," J. of the New African Literature, 2 (Fall 1966), 10-15.


364. LARYEA, BOSSMAN, 1910-         Ghana

    Anthologized in:
        Swanzy. Voices of Ghana.


365. LINDSAY, J.K.O., 1933-         Ghana

    Anthologized in:
        Swanzy. Voices of Ghana.

366. LIYONG, TABAN LO                              Uganda

    "The education of Taban lo Liyong," (story) Transition,
    V, 24 (1966), 12-19.


367. LOBA, AKE, 1927-                              Ivory Coast

    Anthologized in:
        Mphahlele. African writing today.


368. LUTHULI, ALBERT, 1899-                        S. Africa

    Let my people go. Intro. Charles Hooper. (autobiography)
        New York: McGraw-Hill, 1962. 255p.
        London: Collins, 1962. 255p.


369. MABONA, MONGAMELI                             S. Africa

    Anthologized in:
        Presence Africaine, no.57.


370. MAIMANE, ARTHUR, 1930-                        S. Africa

    The dung-heap flower. Read at Transcription Centre Theatre
        Workshop, January 1965.

    "The day after," (story) Transition, VI, 27 (1966), 8-12.

    "Kaffer woman," (story) Black Orpheus, 12 (1963), 37-42.

    "A manner of speaking," (story) Africa South in Exile,
        IV, 4 (1960), 113-118.


371. MARKWEI, MATEI                                Ghana

    Anthologized in:
        Hughes. An African treasury.


372. MARTEY, E.K., 1935-                           Ghana

    Anthologized in:
        Swanzy. Voices of Ghana

373. MATSHIKIZA, TODD, 1920-                    S. Africa

    Chocolates for my wife;  slices of my life.  (autobiography)
        London:  Hodder and Stoughton, 1961.  127p.

    Rev:  Salem Okonga, Presence Africaine, Eng. ed., XI, 39
        (1961), 245-246.
      E. Mphahlele, Transition, II, 5 (1962), 24.

    Anthologized in:
        Hughes.  An African Treasury.
        Mphahlele.  African writing today.

374. MATTHEWS, JAMES, 1929-                    S. Africa

    "Azikwelwa!"  (story)  Africa South, III, 1 (1958), 118-123.

    "The park,"  (story)  Presence Africaine, Eng. ed., XVI, 44
    (1962), 95-105.

    "The party,"  (story)  Transition, IV, 10 (1963), 9-12.

    Anthologized in:
        Denny.  Pan African short stories.
        Komey.  Modern African stories.
        Rive.  Modern African prose.
        --.  Quartet.

375. MBITI, JOHN, 1931-                    Kenya

    M. and his story.  (stories)
        London:  Nelson, 1954.  60p.

    "Wavata and the iimu,"  (story)  Presence Africaine, Eng. ed.,
    IV-V, 32-33 (1960), 146-148.

    Anthologized in:
        Moore.  Modern poetry from Africa.
        Presence Africaine, no.57.

376.  MBOYA, TOM, 1930–                        Kenya

  Freedom and after. (essay)
    London:  Deutsch, 1963.  x, 288p.
    Boston:  Little, Brown, 1963.  x, 288p.

  Rev:  TLS, 18 October 1963, p.818.


377.  MENSAH, ALBERT W. KAYPER, 1923–        Ghana

  Light in jungle Africa. (verse)
    Margaret Wrong prize, 1956.

  Anthologized in:
    Reed.  A book of African verse.
    Swanzy.  Voices of Ghana.


378.  MENSAH, G.M.K., 1935–                  Ghana

  Anthologized in:
    Swanzy.  Voices of Ghana.


379.  MENSAH, J.V., 1935–                    Ghana

  Anthologized in:
    Swanzy.  Voices of Ghana.


380.  MILNER-BROWN, A.L.                      Ghana

  Anthologized in:
    Hughes.  Poems from black Africa.


381.  MKAPA, BEN                             Tanzania

  Anthologized in:
    Cook.  Origin East Africa.

82. MODISANE, WILLIAM (BLOKE), 1923-        S. Africa

    Blame me on history. (autobiography)
        New York: Dutton, 1963. 311p.
        London: Thames and Hudson, 1963. 311p.


    The dignity of begging. (story)
        Johannesburg: Drum Publications, 1951.


    "The professional beggar," (story) West African Review,
       XXXII (March 1962), 57-61.

    "The situation," (story) Black Orpheus, 12 (1963), 10-16.


    Anthologized in:
        Hughes. An African treasury.
        --. Poems from black Africa.
        Rutherfoord. African voices.


383. MODUPE, PRINCE, 1890-                    Guinea

    I was a savage. (autobiography)
        London: Museum Press, 1958. 168p. Foreword Elspeth
        Huxley. Illus. Rosemary Grimble.

    Rev: Ulli Beier, Black Orpheus, 6 (1959), 54-55.


    Anthologized in:
        Edwards. West African narrative.
        Tibble. African/English literature.


384. MOORE, BAI TAMIA, 1916-                Liberia

    Ebony dust. (verse)
        Liberia, 1963.


385. MOPELI-PAULUS, ATTWELL SIDWELL, 1913- Basutoland

    Blanket boy (novel)
        New York: Crowell, 1953. vii, 309p. [With Peter
        Lanham]

Blanket boy's moon. (novel)
>London: Collins, 1953. 320p. [With Peter Lanham]

Turn to the dark. (novel)
>London: Jonathan Cape, 1956. 287p. [With Miriam Basner]

386. MOREL, MARION                              S. Africa

Anthologized in:
>Hughes. An African treasury.

387. MOTSISI, CASEY                             S. Africa

"Riot," (story) Classic, I, 2 (1963), 69-74.

"A very important appointment," (story) Classic, I, 1 (1963), 41-50.

Anthologized in:
>Denny. Pan African short stories.
>Komey. Modern African stories.

388. MPHAHLELE, EZEKIEL, 1919-                   S. Africa

Down Second Avenue. (autobiography)
>London: Faber, 1959. 222p.
>Berlin: Seven Seas, 1962. 222p.
>London: Faber, 1965. 183p.

Rev: Diana Speed, Black Orpheus, 6 (1959), 47-48.
>Holman Jameson, Presence Africaine, Eng. ed., XI, 39 (1961), 245.

In corner B. (stories)
>Nairobi: East African Publishing House (Modern African Library), 1967.

The living and the dead, and other stories.
>Ibadan: Ministry of Education, 1961. 66p. Illus. Peter Clarke.

Man must live, and other stories.
       Cape Town:  African Bookman, 1946.
       Ibadan:  Ministry of Education, 1958.


"He and the cat," (story) Classic, I, 1 (1963), 18-23.

"In corner B," (story) Classic, I, 3 (1963), 10-21.

"On the long road; from an African autobiography," Encounter,
   XXII, 2 (February 1964), 41-45.

"The suitcase," (story) Black Orpheus, 4 (1958), 24-28.


Anthologized in:
       Denny.  Pan African short stories.
       Hughes.  An African treasury.
         --.  Poems from black Africa.
       Komey.  Modern African stories.
       Mphahlele.  African writing today.
       Rive.  Modern African prose.
       Tibble.  African/English literature.
       Whiteley.  A selection of African prose.


389.  MUNONYE, JOHN, 1929-                Nigeria

      The only son.  (novel)
          London:  Heinemann, 1966.  201p.
          London:  Heinemann (African Writers Series, no.21)
            1966.

      Rev:  TLS, 21 July 1966, p.629.


390.  MURRAY, A.A.                S. Africa

      The blanket.  (novel)
          New York:  Vanguard, 1958.  192p.

391.  MUTIGA, JOSEPH G., 1940-          Kenya

    "The prisoners," (story) <u>Penpoint</u>, 16 (1964), 33-34.

    <u>Anthologized in</u>:
        Cook.  <u>Origin East Africa</u>
        Tibble.  <u>African/English literature</u>.

392.  MWALILINO, KATOKI          Malawi

    <u>Anthologized in</u>:
        <u>Presence Africaine</u>, no.57.

393.  NAGENDA, JOHN, 1938-          Uganda

    <u>Anthologized in</u>:
        Cook.  <u>Origin East Africa</u>.
        Denny.  <u>Pan African short stories</u>.

394.  NAKASA, NAT, 1937-1965.          S. Africa

    [Essays], <u>Classic</u>, II, 1 (1966), 17-77.

395.  NAZARETH, PETER

    <u>Anthologized in</u>:
        Cook.  <u>Origin East Africa</u>.

396.  NDLOVU, JOSHUA          S. Rhodesia

    "Not enough," (story) <u>J. of the New African Literature</u>,
    1 (Spring 1966), 58-63.

397.  NGUGI, JAMES, 1938-          Kenya

    <u>The black hermit</u>. (drama)
        Makerere University Press, 1963.

    Rev:  G. Moore, <u>Transition</u>, III, 8 (1963), 34.

<u>A grain of wheat</u>. (novel)
     London: Heinemann (African Writers Series, no.36),
       1967.

<u>The river between</u>. (novel)
     London: Heinemann, 1965. 174p.
     London: Heinemann (African Writers Series, no.17),
       1966. 175p.
     Evanston: Northwestern University Press, 1967. 175p.

Rev: W.M. Kelley, <u>African Forum</u>, I, 3 (Winter 1965), 112-113.
     M.M. Carlin, <u>Transition</u>, IV, 19 (1965), 52-53.
     Austin Shelton, <u>Africa Report</u>, XI, 5 (May 1966), 66.
     Edgar Wright, <u>Transition</u>, V, 25 (1966), 52-54.

<u>Weep not, child</u>. (novel)
     London: Heinemann, 1964. 154p.
     London: Heinemann (African Writers Series, no.7),
       1964. 153p.
     Evanston: Northwestern University Press, 1967. 154p.

Rev: A. Irele, <u>Presence Africaine</u>, Eng. ed., XXIV, 52
       (1964), 234-237.
     D.E.S. Maxwell, <u>Black Orpheus</u>, 16 (1964), 59.
     J. Nagenda, <u>Makerere J.</u>, 10 (1964), 69-71.
     <u>TLS</u>, 14 May 1964, p.409.
     M.M. Carlin, <u>Transition</u>, IV, 18 (1965), 53-54.
     B. Lindfors, <u>Books Abroad</u>, XXXIX, 1 (1965), 106.

"The wind," (story) <u>Penpoint</u>, 10 (1961), 9.

<u>Anthologized in</u>:
     Cook. <u>Origin East Africa</u>.
     Denny. <u>Pan African short stories</u>.
     Komey. <u>Modern African stories</u>.
     Ridout. <u>Adjustments</u>.
     Rive. <u>Modern African prose</u>.
     Tibble. <u>African/English literature</u>.
     Whiteley. <u>A selection of African prose</u>.

<u>Criticism</u>:
     John Reed. "James Ngugi and the African novel," <u>J. of
       Commonwealth Literature</u>, 1 (September 1965), 117-121.

398. NGULUKULU, N.G.                          Tanzania

    Anthologized in:
        Cook. Origin East Africa.


399. NICOL, ABIOSEH (DAVIDSON), 1920-     Sierra Leone

    The truly married woman, and other stories.
        London: Oxford University Press (Three Crowns Book),
        1965. 120p. Illus. J.H. Vandi.

    Two African tales: The leopard hunt, and The devil at
    Yolahun Bridge.
        Cambridge [Eng.] University Press, 1965. 76p. Illus.
        Hassan Bangurah.

    Rev: B. Lindfors, Books Abroad, XL, 4 (Autumn 1966), 488-489.
        Edgar Wright, Transition, V, 25 (1966), 52-54.


    "As the night the day," (story) Presence Africaine, Eng. ed.,
    XXVI, 54 (1965), 224-236.


    Anthologized in:
        Bassir. An anthology of West African verse.
        Edwards. West African narrative.
        Hughes. An African treasury.
          --. Poems from black Africa.
        Komey. Modern African stories.
        Mphahlele. African writing today.
        Reed. A book of African verse.
        Rive. Modern African prose.
        Rutherfoord. African voices.
        Tibble. African/English literature.


    Criticism:
        Robert P. Cobb. "The fiction of Abioseh Nicol," African
        Forum, II, 2 (Fall 1966), 122-123.

400. NJAU, REBECCA                          Kenya

The scar; a tragedy in one act.
       Moshi, Tanzania: Kibo Art Gallery, 1965. 32p.

Rev: B. Lindfors, Books Abroad, XL, 3 (Summer 1966), 360.

"Muma," (story) Presence Africaine, Eng. ed., XXII, 50
    (1964), 225-230.

"The scar," (drama) Transition, III, 8 (1963), 23-28.

Anthologized in:
       Hughes. Poems from black Africa.

401. NKETIA, J.H. KWABENA, 1921-              Ghana

Anthologized in:
       Swanzy. Voices of Ghana.

402. NKOSI, LEWIS, 1935-                     S. Africa

Home and exile. (essays)
       London: Longmans, 1965. 136p.

Rev: John Clare, New African, V, 1 (January 1966), 15.
     TLS, 3 February 1966, p.85.
     William A. Payne, Africa Report, XI, 6 (June 1966),
        66-70.

Rhythm of violence. (drama)
       London: Oxford University Press (Three Crowns Book),
       1964. 69p.

Rev: TLS, 13 August 1964, p.728.
     B. Lindfors, Books Abroad, XXXIX, 3 (Summer 1965), 368.

"As for living," (story) New African, V, 5 (June 1966),
    103-105.

"The hotel room," (story) Contrast, II, 3 (1963-64), 53-63.

"The promise," (story) Classic, I, 1 (1963), 24-32.

Anthologized in:
    Mphahlele.  African writing today.


403.  NTANTALA, PHYLLIS               S. Africa

    Anthologized in:
        Hughes.  An African treasury.


404.  NWANKWO, NKEM, 1936-          Nigeria

    Danda.  (novel)
        London: Deutsch, 1964.  205p.

    Rev:  O.R. Dathorne, Black Orpheus, 18 (1965), 59-60.
        Emanuel Obiechina, Nigeria Magazine, 84 (1965), 61-63.
        Thomas Cassirer, African Forum, I, 4 (Spring 1966),
           128.

    Eroya;  a play.
        Ibadan:  1963.  23p.


    Tales out of school.  (juvenilia)
        Lagos:  African Universities Press (African Reader's
           Library, no.2), 1964.  2d ed. rev. 80p.

    "The gambler," (story) Black Orpheus, 9 (1961), 49-54.

    "His mother," (story) Nigeria Magazine, 80 (1964), 58-60.

    "The man who lost," (story) Nigeria Magazine, 84 (1965),
        68-72.


    Anthologized in:
        Ademola.  Reflections.
        Komey.  Modern African stories.
        Tibble.  African/English literature.


405.  NWANODI, OKOGBULE GLORY, 1936-     Nigeria

    Icheke, and other poems.
        Ibadan: Mbari, 1964.  31p.

Rev: Bona Onyejeli, Nigeria Magazine, 84 (1965), 63-64.
Theo Vincent, Black Orpheus, 18 (1965), 58-59.


406. NWAPA, FLORA, 1931-                    Nigeria

Efuru. (novel)
    London: Heinemann, 1966. 281p.
    London: Heinemann (African Writers Series, no.26), 1966.

Rev: TLS, 7 April 1966, p.281.
    Caroline Ifeka, Nigeria Magazine, 89 (1966), 131-132.


407. NWEKE, CHUBA                           Nigeria

Anthologized in:
    Hughes. Poems from black Africa.


408. NYAKU, FRANK KOFI, 1924-              Ghana

Anthologized in:
    Swanzy. Voices of Ghana.


409. NZEKWU, ONUORA, 1928-                 Nigeria

Blade among the boys. (novel)
    London: Hutchinson, 1962.
    London: Arrow Books, 1964. 191p.

Rev: TLS, 10 August 1962, p.571.
    Kaye Whiteman, Presence Africaine, Eng. ed., XXII,
    50 (1964), 281-283.


Eze goes to school, by Onuora Nzekwu and Michael Crowder.
    (juvenilia)
    Lagos: African Universities Press (African Reader's
    Library, no.4), 1963. 79p.


Highlife for lizards. (novel)
    London: Hutchinson, 1965. 192p.

Rev: M.J.C. Echeruo, Nigeria Magazine, 87 (1965).

Wand of noble wood. (novel)
    London: Hutchinson, 1961. 208p.
    New York: New American Library (Signet D2262), 1966.
        142p.

Rev: O. Aragbalu, Black Orpheus, 11 (1962), 66-67.
     K. Whiteman, Presence Africaine, Eng. ed., XXII, 50
        (1964), 281-283.

Anthologized in:
    Ademola. Reflections.
    Mphahlele. African writing today.
    Rive. Modern African prose.
    Tibble. African/English literature.

410. OBIKA, FRANCIS                    Nigeria

    Anthologized in:
        Rutherfoord. African voices.

411. ODEKU, E. LATUNDE                 Nigeria

    Twilight out of the night.
        Ibadan: University of Ibadan Press, 1964. 139p.

412. OFORI, HENRY, 1924-              Ghana

    Anthologized in:
        Swanzy. Voices of Ghana.

413. OGOT, GRACE A., 1930-            Kenya

    The promised land. (novel)
        Nairobi: East African Publishing House (Modern African
        Library), 1967.

    "Elizabeth," (story) East Africa Journal (September 1966), 11-18.

    "Ward nine," (story) Transition, III, 13 (1964), 41-45.

    "The year of sacrifice," (story) Black Orpheus, 11 (1962),
        41.

Anthologized in:
 Denny. Pan African short stories.
 Komey. Modern African stories.
 Mphahlele. African writing today.

414. OGUNYEMI, WALE                        Nigeria

 Business express. (drama)
        Oshogbo: Theatre Express Sketches, 1966.  30p.


415. OKAFOR, MICHAEL

 "Jigida, or the string of beads," (story) Black Orpheus,
    9 (1961), 22-24.


416. OKAFOR-OMALI, DILIM, 1927-            Nigeria

 A Nigerian villager in two worlds. (biography)
        London: Faber, 1965.  159p.

 Rev: D.A.N. Jones, New Statesman, 9 April 1965, p.577.
      TLS, 29 July 1965, p.655.


417. OKARA, GABRIEL IMOMOTIMI, 1921-       Nigeria

 The voice. (novel)
        London: Deutsch, 1964.  157p.

 Rev: TLS, 17 September 1964, p.853.
      Wilfred Cartey, African Forum, I, 2 (Fall 1965), 110-112.
      M. Macmillan, J. of Commonwealth Literature, 1
        (September 1965), 174-175.
      E. Wright, East Africa Journal (May 1965), 37-38.
      Sunday O. Anozie, Bulletin of the Association for African
        Literature in English, 3 (1965), 54-67.
      Ulli Beier, Black Orpheus, 17 (1965), 60-61.
      Emanuel Obiechina, Nigeria Magazine, 84 (1965), 61-63.

 "The crooks," (story) Black Orpheus, 8 (1960), 6-8.

Anthologized in:
    Ademola. Reflections.
    Denny. Pan African short stories.
    Hughes. An African treasury.
    --. Poems from black Africa.
    Komey. Modern African stories.
    Moore. Modern poetry from Africa.
    Reed. A book of African verse.
    Tibble. African/English literature.

418. OKIGBO, CHRISTOPHER, 1932-        Nigeria

Heavensgate. (verse)
    Ibadan: Mbari, 1962. 39p. Illus. Demas Nwoko.

Rev: Ulli Beier, Black Orpheus, 12 (1963), 46-50.

Limits. (verse)
    Ibadan: Mbari, 1964.

Rev: O.R. Dathorne, Black Orpheus, 15 (1964), 59-60.
    M. Rukeyser, African Forum, I, 1 (Summer 1965), 145-148.

Anthologized in:
    Ademola. Reflections.
    Hughes. Poems from black Africa.
    Moore. Modern poetry from Africa.
    Reed. A book of African verse.
    Tibble. African/English literature.

Criticism:
    Paul Theroux. Transition, V, 22 (1965), 18-20.

419. OKOGIE, M.O.        Nigeria

Songs of Africa. (verse)
    Ilfracombe, Devonshire: Stockwell, 1961. 47p.

420. OKONKWO, NATHAN N.D.        Nigeria

"Udenze's twitching muscle," (story) Nigeria Magazine, 85
(1965), 132-135.

421.  OKOT, J.O. P'BITEK                Uganda

    Song of Lawino.
          Nairobi: East African Publishing House, 1967.

    Rev: TLS, 16 February 1967, p.125.


422.  OKOYE, MOKWUGO, 1926-            Nigeria

    Some facts and fancies. (essays and verse)
          Yaba, Nigeria: Author, 1953. 52p.


    Vistas of life.
          Onitsha: Author, 1962. 228p.


423.  OKPAKU, JOSEPH O.O.             Nigeria

    "Born astride the grave," (drama) J. of the New African
    Literature, 1 (Spring 1966), 21-57.

    "The hole in the dark," (story) J. of the New African
    Literature, 1 (Spring 1966), 69-73.


424.  OLAGOKE, D. OLU                 Nigeria

    The incorruptible judge.
          London: Evans Brothers (Plays for African Schools),
          1962. 48p.

    The iroko-man and the wood carver.
          London: Evans Brothers (Plays for African Schools),
          1963. 44p.


425.  OLEGHE, PIOUS                   Nigeria

    Anthologized in:
          Banham. Nigerian student verse.
          Reed. A book of African verse.

426.  ONADIPE, KOLA                        Nigeria

    The adventures of Souza, the village lad.  (juvenilia)
        Lagos:  African Universities Press (African Reader's
        Library, no.5), 1964.  2d rev. ed.  92p.  Illus.
        Adebayo Ajayi.


    Sugar girl.  (juvenilia)
        Lagos:  African Universities Press (African Junior
        Library, no.1), 1964.  91p.


427.  ONWUZULIGBO, PETER UDECKUKWU            Nigeria

    Short Igbo stories for the young.
        Onitsha:  Eastern Niger Press, 1957.  29p.


428.  OPARA, RALPH CHUKUEMEKA, 1933-            Nigeria

    Anthologized in:
        Ademola.  Reflections.
        Banham.  Nigerian student verse.


429.  OPOKU, ANDREW AMANKWA, 1912-            Ghana

    Anthologized in:
        Hughes.  Poems from black Africa.
        Swanzy.  Voices of Ghana.


430.  OSADEBAY, DENNIS CHUKUDE, 1911-            Nigeria

    Africa sings.  (verse)
        Ilfracombe, Devonshire:  Stockwell, 1952.  104p.


    Anthologized in:
        Bassir.  An anthology of West African verse.
        Hughes.  Poems from black Africa.


    Criticism:
        Sunday O. Anozie.  "Two Nigerian poets,"  African
        Writer, I, 1 (August 1962), 3-4.  [Osadebay and Clark]

431. OTOO, S.K., 1910-                                Ghana

    Anthologized in:
        Swanzy. Voices of Ghana.


432. OWOYELE, DAVID                                   Nigeria

    Anthologized in:
        Ademola. Reflections.
        Komey. Modern African stories.


433. PARKES, FRANCIS ERNEST KOBINA, 1932- Ghana

    Songs from the wilderness. (verse)
        London: University of London Press, 1965. 64p.


    "A deluge of love," (story) Okyeame, I (January 1961),
    16-20.


    Anthologized in:
        Hughes. An African treasury.
        --. Poems from black Africa.
        Presence Africaine, no. 57.
        Reed. A book of African verse.
        Swanzy. Voices of Ghana.


434. PEDEREK, SIMON                                   Ghana

    Anthologized in:
        Hughes. An African treasury.


435. PEREIRA, FRANCESCA YETUNDE, 1933-         Nigeria

    Anthologized in:
        Hughes. Poems from black Africa.


436. PETERS, LENRIE, 1932-                           Gambia

    Poems.
        Ibadan: Mbari, 1964. 44p.

Rev:  Arthur Drayton,  Black Orpheus, 19 (1966), 57-58.


Satellites.  (verse)
    London:  Heinemann (African Writers Series, no.37), 1967.


The second round.  (novel)
    London:  Heinemann, 1965.  192p.
    London:  Heinemann (African Writers Series, no.22), 1966.
      193p.

Rev:  G. Moore,  East Africa Journal (November 1965), 40.
    B. Lindfors,  Books Abroad, XL, 2 (Spring 1966), 233.
    Charles Larson,  Africa Report, XI, 8 (November 1966), 58.
    J. Reed,  J. of Commonwealth Literature, 2 (December 1966),
      172-173.
    O.R. Dathorne,  Black Orpheus, 19 (1966), 55-56.


Anthologized in:
    Moore.  Modern poetry from Africa.
    Mphahlele.  African writing today.
    Reed.  A book of African verse.
    Tibble.  African/English literature.

437.  RADITLADI, L.D.               Bechuanaland

    Anthologized in:
        Rutherfoord.  African voices.


438.  RIVE, RICHARD, 1931-          S. Africa

    African songs.  (stories)
        Berlin:  Seven Seas, 1963.  149p.

    Rev:  TLS,  20 September 1963, p.709.
        Lewis Nkosi,  Classic, I, 2 (1963), 41-42.
        B. Lindfors,  Books Abroad, XXXIX, 2 (Spring 1965),
          240.


    Emergency.  (novel)
        London:  Faber, 1964.  251p.

Rev: <u>TLS</u>, 12 November 1964, p.1016.
Wilfred Cartey, <u>African Forum</u>, I, 3 (Winter 1966),
115-121.
Christine Obumselu, <u>Black Orpheus</u>, 19 (1966), 59.


"Moon over District Six," (story) <u>Transition</u>, III, 8
(1963), 11.

"North-wester," (story) <u>Contrast</u>, I, 1 (1960), 46-53.

"The party," (story) <u>Classic</u>, I, 1 (1963), 68-76.

"Resurrection," (story) <u>Presence Africaine</u>, Eng. ed., XX,
48 (1963), 124-132.


<u>Anthologized in</u>:
Denny. <u>Pan African short stories</u>.
Hughes. <u>An African treasury</u>.
    --. <u>Poems from black Africa</u>.
Komey. <u>Modern African stories</u>.
Mphahlele. <u>African writing today</u>.
Rive. <u>Modern African prose</u>.
    --. <u>Quartet</u>.
Rutherfoord. <u>African voices</u>.


<u>Criticism</u>:
Bernth Lindfors. "Form and technique in the novels of
Richard Rive and Alex LaGuma," <u>J. of the New African
Literature</u>, 2 (Fall 1966), 10-15.
Edgar Wright. <u>Transition</u>, V, 25 (1966), 52-54.


439. RUBADIRI, DAVID, 1930-          Malawi

<u>No bride price</u>. (novel)
Nairobi: East African Publishing House (Modern African
Library), 1967.


"Come to tea," (drama) <u>New African</u>, IV, 5 (July 1965),
106-107.

Anthologized in:
    Cook. <u>Origin East Africa</u>.
    Hughes. <u>Poems from black Africa</u>.
    Moore. <u>Modern poetry from Africa</u>.
    <u>Presence Africaine</u>, no.57.
    Reed. <u>A book of African verse</u>.
    Rutherfoord. <u>African voices</u>.

440. SEGUN, MABEL                   Nigeria

    <u>My father's daughter</u>. (juvenilia)
        Lagos: African University Press (African Reader's
          Library, no.8), 1965. 80p. Illus. Prue Theobalds.

    Anthologized in:
        Ademola. <u>Reflections</u>.

441. SEHUME, LESLIE                S. Africa

    "I'm not a tramp," (story) <u>Classic</u>, I, 1 (1963), 33-38.

442. SELORMEY, FRANCIS, 1927-        Ghana

    <u>The narrow path</u>. (novel)
        London: Heinemann, 1966. 183p.
        New York: Praeger, 1966. 183p.

    Rev: <u>TLS</u>, 21 July 1966, p.629.
        <u>New Statesman</u>, 22 July 1966, p.136.
        Alfred Hutchinson, <u>New African</u>, V, 8 (October 1966), 168.

    "The witch," (story) <u>Okyeame</u>, II, 2 (June 1965), 42-47.

    Anthologized in:
        Edwards. <u>West African narrative</u>.

443. SETSOAFIA, H.K.B., 1920-        Ghana

    Anthologized in:
        Swanzy. <u>Voices of Ghana</u>.

444. SEY, K. ABAKA                          Ghana

    "A father's salvation," (story) <u>Presence Africaine</u>, Eng.
    ed., XII, 40 (1962), 65-70.


445. SINAH, M.W., 1923-                      Sierra Leone

    <u>Anthologized in:</u>
        Rutherfoord. <u>African voices</u>.


446. SMITH, J. AGGREY, 1921-                 Ghana

    <u>Anthologized in:</u>
        Swanzy. <u>Voices of Ghana</u>.


447. SOFOLA, SAMUEL ADENIYI                  Nigeria

    <u>When a philosopher falls in love.</u> (drama)
        New York: Comet Press, 1956. 200p.


448. SOFOWOTE, SEGUN                         Nigeria

    <u>Sailor boy in town</u>. (drama)
        Oshogbo: Theatre Express Sketches, 1966. 26p.


449. SOLARIN, TAI                            Nigeria

    <u>Thinking with you</u>. (essays)
        Ikeja: Longmans of Nigeria, 1965. 100p.

    Rev: Suzanne Cronje, <u>New African</u>, V, 2 (March 1966), 35.


450. SOYINKA, WOLE, 1935-                    Nigeria

    <u>Before the blackout</u>. (satiric revue)
        Performed Ibadan, 1965.

    <u>A dance of the forests</u>. (drama)
        London: Oxford University Press (Three Crowns Book),
        1963. 89p.

Rev: Ulli Beier, Black Orpheus, 8 (1960), 57-58.
Ian Watson, Transition, VI, 27 (1966), 24-26.


Five plays: A dance of the forests; The lion and the jewel;
The swamp dwellers; The trials of Brother Jero; The strong
breed.
    London: Oxford University Press, 1964. 276p.

Rev: Geoffrey Hill, J. of Commonwealth Literature, 1 (September
    1965), 172-174.
E. Wright, East Africa Journal (November 1965), 35-38.
TLS, 1 April 1965, p.252.
M. Esslin, Black Orpheus, 19 (1966), 33-39.


The interpreters. (novel)
    London: Deutsch, 1965. 253p.

Rev: Gerald Moore, Inkululeko, I, 3 (September 1965), 56.
Gerald Moore, New African, IV, 7 (September 1965), 156.
John Thompson, African Forum, I, 2 (Fall 1965), 108-109.
I.N.C. Aniebo, Nigeria Magazine, 86 (1965), 218-220.
Donatus Nwoga, Ibadan, 22 (June 1966), 62-63.
Eldred Jones, Bulletin of the Association for African
    Literature in English, 4 (1966), 13-18.
Bruce King, Black Orpheus, 19 (1966), 55.


Kongi's harvest (drama)
    London: Oxford University Press (Three Crowns Book),
    1967.


The lion and the jewel. (drama)
    London: Oxford University Press (Three Crowns Book),
    1963. 64p.

Rev: Peter Nazareth, Transition, IV, 10 (1963), 47-48.
Ronald Bryden, Observer, 18 December 1966, p.20.


The road. (drama)
    London: Oxford University Press (Three Crowns Book),
    1965. 101p.

Rev: <u>TLS</u>, 10 June 1965, p.476.
     <u>Observer</u>, 19 September 1965.
     C. Pieterse, <u>Cultural Events in Africa</u>, 10 (September
       1965), 4-5.
     Austin Shelton, <u>Africa Report</u>, XI, 5 (May 1966), 66.
     Bernice Duncan, <u>Books Abroad</u>, XL, 3 (Summer 1966),
       360-361.


<u>Three plays: The swamp-dwellers; The trials of Brother Jero;
The strong breed</u>.
     Ibadan: Mbari, 1963. 118p.

Rev: Akanji, <u>Black Orpheus</u>, 13 (1963), 58-59.
     David Cook, <u>Transition</u>, III, 13 (1964), 38-40.


<u>Anthologized in</u>:
     Ademola. <u>Reflections</u>.
     Hughes. <u>An African treasury</u>.
       --. <u>Poems from black Africa</u>.
     Moore. <u>Modern poetry from Africa</u>.
     Mphahlele. <u>African writing today</u>.
     <u>Presence Africaine</u>, no.57.
     Reed. <u>A book of African verse</u>.
     Tibble. <u>African/English literature</u>.


<u>Criticism</u>:
     Martin Banham. <u>Books Abroad</u>, XXXVIII, 1 (Winter 1964), 92.
     Una MacLean. "Soyinka's international drama," <u>Black
       Orpheus</u>, 15 (1964), 46-51.
     M.M. Mahood (et al). "Three views of <u>The swamp dwellers</u>,"
       <u>Ibadan</u>, 6 (June 1959), 27-28.
     John Povey. "Wole Soyinka and the Nigerian drama,"
       <u>Triquarterly</u>, 5 (1966), 129-135.
     Barry Reckord. "Notes on two Nigerian playwrights,"
       <u>New African</u>, IV, 7 (September 1965), 171. [Clark and
       Soyinka]
     Susan Yankowitz. "The plays of Wole Soyinka," <u>African
       Forum</u>, I, 4 (Spring 1966), 129-133.

451. SUTHERLAND, EFUA THEODORA, 1924-        Ghana

Playtime in Africa. (picture essay)
    New York: Atheneum 1962. 56p.


The roadmakers. (picture essay)
    Accra: Ghana Information Services, 1961. 80p.
    Photographs Willis E. Bell.


"Edufa," (drama) Okyeame, III, 1 (December 1966), 47-49.

"Foruwa," (drama) Okyeame, II, 1 (1964), 40-47.

"Samantaase village," (story) Okyeame, I (January 1961),
    53-58.

"You swore an oath: 'Anasegoro'," (drama) Presence
    Africaine, Eng. ed., XXII, 50 (1964), 231-247.


Anthologized in:
        Bassir. An anthology of West African verse.
        Denny. Pan African short stories.
        Hughes. An African treasury.
        Rive. Modern African prose.
        Swanzy. Voices of Ghana.
        Tibble. African/English literature.


452. THEMBA, CAN, 1924-                    S. Africa

"The suit," (story) Classic, I, 1 (1963), 6-16.


Anthologized in:
        Hughes. An African treasury.
        Komey. Modern African stories.
        Mphahlele. African writing today.
        Rutherfoord. African voices.

453. TUTUOLA, AMOS, 1920-                    Nigeria

The brave African huntress. (novel)
        London: Faber, 1958. 150p. Illus. Ben Enwonwu.

Rev: Akanji, Black Orpheus, 4 (1958), 51-53.


Feather woman of the jungle. (novel)
        London: Faber, 1962. 132p.


My life in the bush of ghosts. (novel)
        London: Faber, 1954, 1964. 174p.
        New York: Grove Press, 1954.

Rev: O.D. Thiam, Presence Africaine, Eng. ed., XXIII, 51
    (1964), 174-175.


The palm-wine drinkard and his dead palm-wine tapster in the
Deads' Town. (novel)
        London: Faber, 1952, 1962. 125p.
        New York: Grove Press, 1953. 130p.

Rev: Eldred Jones, Bulletin of the Association for African
        Literature in English, 4 (1966), 24-30.


Simbi and the satyr of the dark jungle. (novel)
        London: Faber, 1955. 136p.


"Ajayi and the witchdoctor," (story) Black Orpheus, 19 (1966),
    10-14; Atlantic, CCIII, 4 (April 1959), 78-80.

"Don't pay bad for bad," (story) Presence Africaine, Eng. ed.,
    II, 30 (1960), 78-81.

"The duckling brothers and their disobedient sister," (story)
    Presence Africaine, Eng. ed., VIII, 36 (1961), 73-78.


Anthologized in:
        Ademola. Reflections.
        Edwards. West African narrative.
        Hughes. An African treasury.

Komey. <u>Modern African stories</u>.
Mphahlele. <u>African writing today</u>.
Rive. <u>Modern African prose</u>.
Rutherfoord. <u>African voices</u>.
Tibble. <u>African/English literature</u>.
Whiteley. <u>A selection of African prose</u>.

<u>Criticism</u>:
Gerald Moore. "Amos Tutuola," <u>Black Orpheus</u>, 1
(1957), 27-35.

454. UKWU, U.I.                                    Nigeria

<u>Anthologized in</u>:
Banham. <u>Nigerian student verse</u>.
Reed. <u>A book of African verse</u>.

455. UMUKORO, GORDON                               Nigeria

<u>Anthologized in</u>:
Banham. <u>Nigerian student verse</u>.

456. WACIUMA, CHARITY

<u>Daughter of Mumbi</u>. (autobiography)
Nairobi: East African Publishing House (Modern
African Library), 1967.

457. WAIGURU, JOSEPH, 1939-                         Kenya

<u>Anthologized in</u>:
Cook. <u>Origin East Africa</u>.

458. WANNENBURGH, ALF, 1936-                     S. Africa

"Almost home," (story) <u>Black Orpheus</u>, 11 (1962), 58.

"Echoes," (story) <u>Presence Africaine</u>, Eng. ed., XXIV,
52 (1964), 172-176.

"Only a ...," (story) <u>African Writer</u>, I, 1 (August 1962), 19-2

Anthologized in:
    Rive. <u>Modern African prose.</u>
    --. <u>Quartet.</u>

459. WARDY, F.K. CHAPMAN, 1924-        Ghana

    Anthologized in:
        Swanzy. <u>Voices of Ghana.</u>

460. WILLIAMS, DENIS

    "Sperm of God," (notes of a forthcoming novel) <u>Transition,</u>
    28 (1967), 9-13.

461. WILLIAMS, GASTON BART, 1938-        Sierra Leone

    Anthologized in:
        Beier. <u>Black Orpheus anthology.</u>

462. WINFUL, E. ARCHIE, 1922-        Ghana

    Anthologized in:
        Swanzy. <u>Voices of Ghana.</u>

463. ZIRIMU, ELVANIA NAMUKWAYA, 1938-    Uganda

    Anthologized in:
        Cook. <u>Origin East Africa.</u>

Selected periodicals.

Abbia. P.B. 4068, Yaounde, Cameroun.

Africa Report. Suite 500, Dupont Circle Building, Washington, D.C.
          20036.

Africa Today. Graduate School of International Studies, University of
          Denver, University Park Campus, Denver, Colorado  80210.

African Forum. American Society of African Culture, 401 Broadway, New
          York, N.Y.  10013.

African Notes. Bulletin of the Institute of African Studies, University
          of Ibadan, Ibadan, Nigeria.

African Studies Bulletin. Hoover Institution, Stanford University,
          Stanford, California  94305.

Black Orpheus. Longmans of Nigeria, Ltd. in association with Mbari,
          Ibadan. Ikeja, Nigeria.

Books Abroad. University of Oklahoma Press, Norman, Oklahoma  73069.

Bulletin of the Association for African Literature in English.  Departmen
          of English, Fourah Bay College, Freetown, Sierra Leone.

The Classic. Classic Magazine Trust Fund, Box 23642, Joubert Park,
          Johannesburg, S. Africa.

Contrast. Box 3841, Cape Town, South Africa.

Cultural Events in Africa. Transcription Centre, 38 Dover Street,
          London W1, England.

Darlite. Department of Literature, University College, P.O. Box 9184,
          Dar es Salaam, Tanzania.

East Africa Journal. East African Institute of Social and Cultural
          Affairs, Box 30492, Nairobi, Kenya.

English Studies in Africa. Witwatersrand University Press, Johannesburg,
          S. Africa.

Ibadan. University of Ibadan, Ibadan, Nigeria.

Journal of Commonwealth Literature. University of Leeds in association
          with Heinemann Educational Books, Ltd., 48 Charles Street,
          London W1, England.

Journal of Modern African Studies. Cambridge University Press, Bentley
          House, 200 Euston Road, London NW1, England.

Journal of the New African Literature and the Arts. Box 4392, Stanford
          University, Palo Alto, California 94305.

Makerere Journal. Faculty of Arts, Makerere University College, P.O.
          Box 262, Kampala, Uganda.

New African. 60 Paddington Street, London W1, England.

New Statesman. Great Turnstile, London WC1, England.

Nigeria Magazine. Exhibition Centre, Marina, Lagos, Nigeria.

Nigerian Libraries. The Librarian, University of Ibadan, Ibadan, Nigeria.

Okyeame. Writers' Workshop, in collaboration with the Institute of African
          Studies, University of Ghana, Legon, Ghana.

Penpoint. Department of English, Makerere University College, Kampala,
          Uganda.

Phylon. Atlanta University, Atlanta, Georgia  30314.

Presence Africaine. 42 rue Descartes, Paris, France.

Times Literary Supplement. Printing House Square, London EC4, England

Transition. P.O. Box 20026, Kampala, Uganda.

## Author Index

Authors of works and criticism, but not of reviews, are included here.

Note: figures in index refer to entry numbers.

Abasiekong, D.                   138
Abbs, A.                         251
Aboderin, S.F.                   252
Abraham, W.E.                      8
Abrahams, P.                     253
Abruquah, J.W.                   254
Achebe, C.          21, 22, 117
                   163, 171, 255
Adali-Mortti, G.                 256
Addo, J.                         257
Adebayo, Y.                      258
Ademola, F.              292, 231
Adeyemo, G.A.                    259
Agbadja, A.K.A.                  260
Aidoo, C.A.A.                    261
Aig-Imoukhuede, F.A.             262
Aiyegbusi, T.                    263
Ajao, A.                         264
Ajose, A.                        265
Akinsemoyin, K.                  266
Akobo, B.                        267
Akpan, N.U.                      268
Akpoyoware, M.                   269
Aluko, T.M.                      270
Amadi, E.                        271
Amosu, M.                          1
Anang, Michael Dei
   see Dei-Anang, M.
Aniebo, I.N.C.                   272
Annan, K.                        273
Anozie, S.O.             292, 430
Archibald-Aikins, S.E.           274
Arkhurst, F.S.                   275
Armah, A.K.                      276
Asalache, K.                     277
Astrachan, A.M.           25, 292
Awoonor-Williams, G.      26, 278
Axworthy, G.                     327
Babalola, A.                     279
Babatunde
   see Horatio-Jones, E.B.

Banham, M.J.      27, 28, 29, 89
                  105, 106, 232, 450
Bart-Williams
   see Williams, Gaston Bart
Bassir, O.                       233
Bastide, R.                      185
Bedwei, A.                       280
Beier, U.       9, 139, 140, 141
               142, 158, 177, 234, 241
Bereng, M.                       281
Bilen, M.                        143
p'Bitek, Okot
   see Okot, p'Bitek
Blair, D.S.                 186, 187
Blay, J.B.                       282
Bodurin, A.                       31
Boetie, D.                       283
Bondy, S.S.                      284
Bown, L.                          10
Brew, K.                         285
Brown, C.E.                      286
Brutus, D.                       287
Buahin, P.K.                     288
Bulane, M.                       360
Butler, G.                       144
Carroll, D.R.                    122
Chacha, T.                       289
Chijioke, M.                     290
Chukwukere, B.I.            118, 137
Citashe, I.W.W.                  291
Clark, J.P.         107, 145, 146
                    147, 148, 292
Clarke, P.                       293
Cobb, R.P.                       399
Cole, R.W.                       294
Conton, W.                       295
Cook, D.                         235
Crowder, M.           10, 32, 33
Cudjoe, S.D.                     296
Dadson, I.B.                     297
Dathorne, O.R.        34, 108, 119
                                 120

| | |
|---|---|
| deGraft, J.C. | 109, 298 |
| Dei-Anang, M.F. | 35, 299 |
| deMott, B. | 36 |
| Dempster, R.T. | 300 |
| Denny, N. | 236 |
| Derimanu, A.B. | 301 |
| Dipoko, M.S. | 302 |
| Djoleto, S.A.A. | 303 |
| Dove-Danquah, M. | 304 |
| Drachler, J. | 237 |
| Drayton, A.D. | 121 |
| Duodu, M.C. | 305 |
| Easmon, R.S. | 306 |
| Echeruo, M.J.C. | 38, 149, 307 |
| Edwards, Paul | 122, 123, 238 |
| Egbuna, O.B. | 308 |
| Ekpenyong, J.O. | 164 |
| Ekwensi, C. | 39, 40, 41, 309 |
| Ekwere, J.D. | 310 |
| Epelle, S. | 311 |
| Esan, Y. | 312 |
| Esedebe, P.O. | 159 |
| Esslin, M. | 110 |
| Eyakuze, V. | 313 |
| Faleti, A. | 314 |
| Ferguson, J. | 150 |
| Feuser, W. | 188 |
| Fonlon, B. | 217, 218 |
| Furay, M. | 189, 190 |
| Gabre-Mehdin, T. | 315 |
| Gardiner, R.K.A. | 316 |
| Gashe, Marina | |
| see Njau, Rebecca | |
| Gatheru, R.M. | 317 |
| Gatuiria, J. | 318 |
| George, C. | 319 |
| Gerard, A.S. | 124 |
| Ghartey, J. | 320 |
| Gicaru, M. | 321 |
| Gicogo, G. | 322 |
| Gleason, J.I. | 11, 42 |
| Gordimer, N. | 125 |
| Hagan, G.R. | 323 |
| Hall, B. | 324 |
| Hanshell, D. | 43 |

| | |
|---|---|
| Haresnape, G. | 44 |
| Head, B. | 325 |
| Hendrickse, Begum | 181 |
| Henries, A.D.B. | 326 |
| Henshaw, J.E. | 327 |
| Higo, A. | 328 |
| Hihetah, R.K. | 329 |
| Hoh, I.K. | 330 |
| Hokororo, A.M. | 331 |
| Hopkinson, T. | 45 |
| Horatio-Jones, E.B. | 332 |
| Hughes, L. | 239 |
| Hutchinson, A. | 333 |
| Idan, L.K. | 334 |
| Ijimere, O. | 335 |
| Ike, V.C. | 336 |
| Imoukhuede, Mabel | |
| see Segun, Mabel | |
| Irele, A. | 191, 192, 193 |
| | 255, 337 |
| Jabavu, N. | 338 |
| Jahn, J. | 2, 12, 19, 46, 47 |
| | 90, 227 |
| Jeanpierre, W.A. | 194 |
| Johnson, L. | 339 |
| Johnson, W. | 166 |
| Jones, D.A.N. | 48 |
| Jones, Edward Babatunde Horatio | |
| see Horatio-Jones, E.B. | |
| Jones, E.D. | 49, 50, 245, 340 |
| Jones-Quartey, K.B. | 341 |
| Jordan, A.C. | 51, 342 |
| July, R.W. | 52, 160 |
| Kachingwe, A. | 343 |
| Kaggwa, M. | 344 |
| Kaggwa, N. | 161 |
| Kagwe, S. | 345 |
| Kahiga, S. | 354 |
| Kane, Mohamadou | 53 |
| Kariara, J. | 346 |
| Karibo, M. | 347 |
| Karienye, M. | 348 |
| Kariuki, J.E. | 349 |
| Kariuki, J.M. | 350 |
| Kaunda, K.D. | 351 |

| | |
|---|---|
| Kayira, L. | 352 |
| Kennard, P. | 111 |
| Kennedy, E. | 196 |
| Khunga, C. | 353 |
| Kibera, L. | 354 |
| Killam, D. | 54 |
| Kimenye, B. | 355 |
| King, D. | 356 |
| Kokunda, V. | 357 |
| Kolade, C. | 112 |
| Komey, E.A. | 240, 358 |
| Konadu, A. | 359 |
| Kumalo, Peter | |
| see Clarke, Peter | |
| Kunene, R.M. | 360 |
| Kurankyi-Taylor, D. | 361 |
| Kwabena Nketia, J.H. | |
| see Nketia, J.H. Kwabena | |
| Kyei, K.G. | 362 |
| Lagneau-Kesteloot, L. | 172 |
| LaGuma, A. | 363 |
| Laryea, B. | 364 |
| Lienhardt, P. | 55 |
| Lindfors, B. | 56, 57, 126, 127 |
| | 128, 363, 438 |
| Lindsay, J.K.O. | 365 |
| Liyong, Taban lo | 60, 366 |
| Loba, A. | 367 |
| Luthuli, A. | 368 |
| Mabona, M. | 369 |
| McHardy, C. | 113 |
| MacLean, U. | 450 |
| Mahood, M.M. | 450 |
| Maimane, A. | 370 |
| Markwei, M. | 371 |
| Martey, E.K. | 372 |
| Mathew, G. | 61 |
| Matshikiza, T. | 373 |
| Matthews, J. | 374 |
| Mazisi, Raymond | |
| see Kunene, Raymond Mazisi | |
| Mbiti, J. | 375 |
| Mboya, T. | 376 |
| Melone, T. | 197 |
| Mensah, A.W.K. | 377 |
| Mensah, G.M.K. | 378 |
| Mensah, J.V. | 379 |
| Mezu, S.O. | 151 |

| | |
|---|---|
| Milner-Brown, A.L. | 380 |
| Mkapa, B. | 381 |
| Modisane, W. (Bloke) | 219, 382 |
| Modupe, Prince | 383 |
| Moore, B.T. | 384 |
| Moore, G. | 13, 14, 62, 63 |
| | 64, 152, 208, 230, 241, 453 |
| Mopeli-Paulus, A.S. | 385 |
| Morel, M. | 386 |
| Morgue, Efua | |
| see Sutherland, Efua T. | |
| Motsisi, C. | 387 |
| Mphahlele, E. | 15, 65, 66, 67 |
| | 68, 167, 182, 198, 206 |
| | 209, 220, 240, 242, 388 |
| Munonye, J. | 389 |
| Murray, A.A. | 390 |
| Mutiga, J.G. | 391 |
| Mwalilino, K. | 392 |
| Nagenda, J. | 221, 393 |
| Nakasa, N. | 69, 394 |
| Nazareth, P. | 71, 395 |
| Ndlovu, J. | 396 |
| Ngugi, J. | 397 |
| Ngulukulu, N.G. | 398 |
| Nicol, A. (Davidson) | 16, 73, 74 |
| | 153, 399 |
| Njau, R. | 400 |
| Nketia, J.H. Kwabena | 401 |
| Nkosi, L. | 75, 76, 77, 78 |
| | 79, 80, 81, 402 |
| Ntantala, P. | 403 |
| Nwankwo, N. | 404 |
| Nwanodi, O.G. | 405 |
| Nwapa, F. | 406 |
| Nweke, C. | 407 |
| Nwoga, D.I. | 178 |
| Nyaku, F.K. | 408 |
| Nzekwu, O. | 212, 409 |
| Obika, F. | 410 |
| Obumselu, B. | 82 |
| Odeku, E.L. | 411 |
| Ofori, H. | 412 |
| Ogot, G. | 413 |
| Ogunba, O. | 114 |
| Ogunyemi, W. | 414 |
| Okafor, M. | 415 |
| Okafor-Omali, D. | 416 |

Okara, G.                           83, 417
Okigbo, C.                              418
Okogie, M.O.                            419
Okonkwo, N.                             420
Okot, p'Bitek                       84, 421
Okoye, M.                               422
Okpaku, J.O.O.                          423
Okwu, E.C.                              168
Olagoke, D.O.                           424
Oleghe, P.                              425
Onadipe, K.                             426
Onwuzuligbo, P.U.                       427
Opara, R.C.                             428
Opoku, A.A.                             429
Osadebay, D.C.                          430
Otoo, S.K.                              431
Owoyele, D.                             432
Parkes, F.E.K.                          433
Parry, J.                               129
Partridge, A.C.                          85
p'Bitek, Okot
   see Okot, p'Bitek
Pederek, S.                             434
Pereira, F.Y.                           435
Peters, L.                              436
Porter, D.                        3, 4, 5, 6
Povey, J.F.       86, 87, 130, 169
                175, 213, 214, 309, 450
Press, J.                                17
Raditladi, L.D.                         437
Ramsaran, J.A.        7, 18, 19, 47
                         88, 89, 90
Reckord, B.              115, 450, 292
Redding S.                               91
Reed, J.                   131, 244, 397
Ridout, R.                              245
Rive, R.          199, 207, 222, 246
                                        438
Rubadiri, D.                        92, 439
Rutherfoord, P.                         247
Schmidt, N.J.                           179
Segal, P.                          176, 223
Segun, M.                               440
Sehume, L.                              441
Selormey, F.                            442
Senanu, K.E.                             93

Senghor, L.S.      201, 202, 215
Setsoafia, H.K.B.                       443
Sey, K.A.                               444
Shelton, A.J.     94, 95, 96, 162
                     200, 255, 309
Shore, H.                               116
Simon, E.                               203
Sinah, M.W.                             445
Smith, J.A.                             446
Sofola, S.A.                            447
Sofowote, S.                            448
Solarin, T.                             449
Soyinka, W.           98, 154, 450
Staniland, M.                           132
Sterling, T.                             99
Stuart, D.                          64, 208
Sutherland, E.T.                        451
Swanzy, H.                              248
Themba, C.                              452
Theroux, P.                        155, 418
Thomas, L.V.                            204
Thomas, P.                              156
Tibble, A.                              249
Tolson, M.                              157
Treadgold, M.                           133
Trout, P.J.                             196
Tucker, M.            134, 135, 136
Tutuola, A.                             453
Ukwu, U.I.                              454
Ulansky, G.                             183
Waciuma, C.                             456
Waiguru, J.                             457
Wake, C.H.            100, 173, 244
Wali, O.                           101, 137
Wannenburgh, A.                         458
Wardy, F.K.C.                           459
Warner, A.                              170
Warren, Y.                              299
Wauthier, C.                             20
Whiteley, W.H.                     102, 250
Williams, D.                       184, 460
Williams, G.B.                          461
Williams, George Awoonor
   see Awoonor-Williams, George
Winful, E.A.                            462
Wonodi
   see Nwanodi, G.O.

Wright, E.            174, 438
Yankowitz, S.              450
Young, P.                  180
Zirimu, E.N.               463